Richard M. Nixon

Herbert S. Parmet

Richard M. Nixon
An American Enigma

THE LIBRARY OF AMERICAN BIOGRAPHY

Series Editor Mark C. Carnes

New York   San Francisco   Boston
London   Toronto   Sydney   Tokyo   Singapore   Madrid
Mexico City   Munich   Paris   Cape Town   Hong Kong   Montreal

Executive Editor: Michael Boezi
Executive Marketing Manager: Sue Westmoreland
Editorial Assistant: Vanessa Gennarelli
Production Coordinator: Scarlett Lindsay
Text Design and Electronic Page Makeup: Alison Barth Burgoyne
Cover Designer/Manager: John Callahan
Cover Image: Getty Images, Inc.
Frontispiece Image: Time & Life Pictures/Getty Images
Manufacturing Manager: Mary Fischer

Library of Congress Cataloging-in-Publication Data

Parmet, Herbert S.
    Richard Nixon : an American enigma / Herbert S. Parmet.
       p. cm. -- (The library of American biography)
    Includes bibliographical references and index.
    ISBN-13: 978-0-321-39893-2
    ISBN-10: 0-321-39893-9
    1. Nixon, Richard M. (Richard Milhous), 1913–1994. 2.
Presidents--United States--Biography. 3. United States--Politics and
government--1969–1974. 4. United States--Politics and government--
1945–1989. I. Title.

E856.P349 2008
973.924092--dc22
[B]   2007034706

Visit us at www.ablongman.com

ISBN-13: 978-0-321-39893-2
ISBN-10:   0-321-39893-9

In memory of Marie B. Hecht, friend and colleague for so many vital years

Contents

Editor's Preface

Richard M. Nixon was this nation's most intriguing president.

The adjective is chosen with care. From the start, Nixon inhabited a world of intrigue: as a soldier in the South Pacific, he won a small fortune as a guileful poker player; his first claim to fame was ferreting out Alger Hiss, a Harvard-educated American diplomat who likely spied for the Soviet Union; as president, Nixon bugged one of his own advisers and compiled lists of enemies; his diplomacy—culminating in a stunning overture to Communist China—was conducted with consummate secrecy; and his downfall occurred after his henchmen had burglarized the headquarters of his political foes, entangling him in a vast web of skullduggery and deceit.

"Intriguing" also connotes "mystery," and this, too, applies with striking force to Nixon. No president was more elusive in his personal relations, more enigmatic in his political stratagems, or more inscrutable in his fundamental motivations. One of his speechwriters, a decade after Nixon's resignation, doubted whether there existed a "real Nixon."

This insight, as this volume shows, generates yet another conundrum. Nixon, though enigmatic, generated a powerful response from friend and foe alike. Many loved him; many hated him. But few knew exactly who he was.

It requires a special sort of sleuth to disperse the fog that has descended upon the historical record, to cast light upon the labyrinthine politics of this troubled era, and to fathom the depths of so complex a character.

Herbert Parmet is such a sleuth. One of the finest historians of the modern American presidency, author of influential biographies of Eisenhower, Kennedy, and George H. W. Bush, among others, Parmet has spent much of the past quarter century in pursuit of the elusive Nixon. In the 1980s, the then-reclusive Nixon, whose natural wariness toward intellectuals had evolved into a political creed, agreed to speak with Parmet; the Nixon–Parmet discussions have added immeasurably to the historical record. Seventeen years ago, he published his first biography of Nixon, a 755-page tome. Now Parmet, Distinguished Professor Emeritus at the City University of New York, provides his summary judgments—along with new revelations. This concise book is a scholarly triumph and a page-turning thriller that gets to the heart of the mystery that was Richard M. Nixon.

MARK C. CARNES

Author's Preface

From the end of World War II until the rise of the New Right, the character of American politics and diplomacy was shaped by the values that were common to the Age of Nixon. It was an age of contention, politically, diplomatically, and culturally, expressed through the prism of the ongoing Cold War. It was, above all, an age of uncertainty about America's role in a confusing and dangerous world.

Richard M. Nixon was certainly among the most enigmatic presidents who ever sat in the White House. He combined the wiles of a Machiavelli, or, as we Americans would prefer, an Ike, the deceptions of an LBJ, the seductive talents of a Reagan, and the conciliatory tendencies of a Ford, Carter, George H. W. Bush, and Clinton. How do we separate his life from where America and Americans have been since World War II?

He was Eisenhower's vice president. When I began my graduate studies at Columbia University in the 1950s, the Cold War was still contentious and far from resolved. The Soviet outerspace achievement, *Sputnik*, was a military and technological challenge. The Eisenhower leadership, then in its dimming days, was starting to unravel, tested by an allied strike at the Suez Canal, a revolt in Hungary, a menacing "Red" China truculent over Formosa and the off-shore islands, the seemingly endless confrontation with the Soviets over the Berlin problem, and the festering inheritance over the residue of French rule in Indochina. With the aging and ill Eisenhower about to run out his second term, the youthful Nixon appeared his logical successor. His leadership promised to revitalize the administration's flagging sharpness.

Sitting in Professor Harold Syrett's graduate seminar on the Federal Period in American history during those days, I was drawn to Aaron Burr as an early personification of the contemporary Richard Nixon. Burr, a central figure in early New York's political wars, a nemesis of Alexander Hamilton, Jefferson's vice president, and the author of a bizarre Southwestern land scheme, became, at least in my mind, Jeffersonian America's Nixon. Richard Nixon, in short, could be understood through the personality and experience of Aaron Burr. I followed through with a graduate school study of the early New Yorker's maneuverings in the election of 1800.

Not until 1984 did I come face to face with the Burr of my original vision, Richard Nixon. I had the good fortune to be granted personal access. Our private sessions in preparation of a biography of the ex-president took place in the federal building on Foley Square in New York City. Nixon's ground rules were clear and acceptable to me: no discussion of Watergate and no tape recorders. I took handwritten notes and dictated others at the end of each session using a micro tape recorder stored in my car. Three long talks in 1984, and meetings with a large number of people in Nixon's world, were later supplemented by some back and forth correspondence with the former president.

Finally, after his office had moved to Woodcliff Lake, New Jersey, and he realized that I was nearing publication, he suggested one last interview. That took place in November 1988, immediately following George H. W. Bush's election to the presidency.

Entering Nixon's new retirement office that day, I was taken aback. He asked whether I had a tape recorder. He clearly had a revised agenda. He now *wanted* to go on tape, dropping his old ground rules. I lamely told him that I had a recorder in my car but very little tape. "Get it," Nixon said, without hesitation. "We can afford more tape."

One of his leading speechwriters later explained that Nixon, always wary of strangers, had developed enough confidence in me to let down his guard. That last session, on November 16, 1988, remains my only recorded interview with Richard Nixon. I was with him for the last time at the Four Seasons Conference in Washington, D.C., in March 1992, and flew to California to attend his funeral two years later.

By then, my first book on Nixon had been published. Also fresh on my mind was a conference on the Eisenhower presidency that I had attended at Gettysburg College in Pennsylvania in October 1990. From my third row seat in the auditorium, next to a prominent veteran Washington journalist, I watched a presentation that included a brief documentary film on those White House years. Seated in front of the screen were several correspondents and veterans of the administration. The most outstanding one in my mind was William P. Rogers. Rogers, then pushing seventy-seven, had been a close and loyal friend to Nixon since the Alger Hiss espionage trial in the 1940s. He had also served as Nixon's first secretary of state. The revealing moment that day at Gettysburg came with the on-screen conclusion of the film that featured Nixon prominently.

When the house lights came on and the clapping began, Rogers, his eye clearly tearful, said to no one in particular but loud enough for us to hear, "I cannot applaud for that man." Thus, in these seconds, we had a vivid confirmation of the Nixon–Kissinger–Rogers tensions that existed within the administration.

Words remain the personal obsessions of authors. But as many generations of writers have demonstrated, woe befalls one so wedded to his creativity that he cannot bear the criticism of others. Only maturity and experience rescue us from the illusion that we can only write our "masterpieces" in rapturous moments of singular inspiration. We then stand before the world with our unique accomplishments unchallenged until, by the light of dawn, we are finally sobered by reality and capable of seeing ourselves as we really are. The more we love our constructions, as Arthur M. Schlesinger, Jr., noted in his final days, the less we can recognize their failings. Others, fortunately, can often see our work more clearly. Some of them have come to my rescue.

That this book would have been written without their help is certain; that it would have been readable is less so. I wish to recognize that simple fact and express my appreciation for the guidance of *Library of American Biography* series editor Mark

Carnes, as well as that of my wise and perceptive wife, Joan Parmet. Irwin Gellman, the author of several fine books, took some valuable time from his own work to spare me self-inflicted embarrassments. His findings gave us laughs instead of tears. To my friend, Jerry T. Tiffany, I would like to extend a belated appreciation for my own image on the jacket of the Bush biography. His creative talents and understanding of the process remained an inspiration for this book. He never let me forget what I was trying to do.

Then there was the band of scholars solicited by my general editor, Michael Boezi of Longman: James Dauphine, Meridian Community College; Ronald B. Frankum, Millersville University of Pennsylvania; Dolph Grundma, Metropolitan State College of Denver; Elsa A. Nystrom, Kennesaw State University; and Gerda W. Ray, University of Missouri, St. Louis.

Editorial assistant Vanessa Gennarelli was always ready when I needed her.

HERBERT S. PARMET

Richard M. Nixon

A Quaker
from Whittier

Richard Milhous Nixon was born in Yorba Linda, California, on January 9, 1913. "Preachers, ministers, shopkeepers" were all part of his background, said his mother, Hannah, but, she added, "I can't think of a Nixon or a Milhous holding an office higher than that of sheriff." They were conventional members of a spiritual community. If there was any departure, it consisted of young Nixon's clear intellectual gifts, a strength for which he would be praised for the rest of his life.

The family's Quaker heritage was intense and dated back to Hannah Milhous's Irish-German ancestors. She, more than most Friends in her part of the country, was a Quaker-style pacifist. A soft-spoken, highly regarded mistress of the household, her name was mentioned almost reverentially. Nixon later remembered her as a spiritual, kind, respected soul, "that everybody loved a very sweet, lovely person that we liked very, very much." On Wednesdays and Sundays, she took the little boy to worship with the strongly puritanical Quaker congregants.

Unlike Hannah, his father, Frank Nixon, was hard working, but a "scrappy, belligerent fighter," whom his son also recalled as on the dark side and combative. Frank, an Ohioan of Scots-Irish parentage and educated

1

in a one-room schoolhouse, worked at whatever he could; he was a streetcar motorman when he met his future wife at a Quaker Valentine's party. He accepted Hannah together with her faith.

Conventional wisdom held that Hannah, already ahead of most contemporary women for having at least attended college, "lowered herself" by marrying Frank Nixon in 1908. She was the daughter of Franklin Milhous, an orchardist who cultivated trees and orange groves and achieved prominence and dignity in the community, even serving on the board of trustees of Whittier College. That, presumably, made him relatively elite by local standards. "The Milhouses thought highly of the Milhouses," someone once sneered, but no one sneered at Frank Nixon because he was "privileged."

He planted lemon trees on a 12-and-a-half-acre tract. It was, the younger Nixon pointed out many years later, "the poorest lemon ranch in California." Only after the land was sold was oil discovered on the property. "And then he was a grocer," his son also reminded a group gathered in the White House in 1974, "but he was a great man. Because he did his job, and every job counts up to the hilt regardless of what happens."

The younger Nixon's early industriousness was clear. He helped run the family store; he also took anything else that came along that others might offer, including lighting smudge pots in the orange groves when frost threatened. He later remembered Whittier as a "small, tight-knit Quaker community" that offered potentially unlimited rewards for "those who were willing to work hard." At the age of seventeen he did his share of pick-up work during summers in Prescott, Arizona, plucking chickens and a serving as a barker at a carnival.

Nixon also had the anguish of seeing two brothers, Arthur and Harold, stricken by disease. Harold, a tubercular patient, required confinement to a nursing home in Arizona. Hannah nursed her son and also helped care for other tubercular patients. Arthur, nine years younger than Harold, died of tubercular encephalitis in 1925, Harold, in 1933.

Those dismal times, especially watching the deaths of two brothers, stuck in Nixon's mind. There were also the rejections, the whistles and catcalls when, as an amateur thespian, he got on the stage to act for the first time; he never forgot his clumsiness on the dance floor with the first girl he really liked. As one of his White House aides later put it, Nixon "was the little kid in the schoolyard all the boys were torturing. In order to escape, he has put on different faces and masks." He was somewhat of a puzzle, or an enigma, even then. Or, as a major biographer later remarked, "It was not easy to be Richard Nixon."

No doubt, by every account, Nixon was a hard worker and a successful student; his mind was sharp and his memory astonishingly retentive. An outstanding primary school student, he went to high schools in East Whittier and Fullerton. Graduating from Whittier High, he finished third. His record included distinction as a debater, becoming the Southern California Intercollegiate Extemporaneous Speaking Champion, an oratorical honor of which he was forever proud. It was his lot, however, to always win more respect than affection for such skills.

In September 1930, when he went on to Whittier College, he became the campus champion of the "nonorgs," or unorganized students. Their Orthogonian Society, as it was named, was contrarian, mostly directed at an outgrowth of an early college debating society, the Franklins, that day's rendition of the sort of Greek letter fraternities that the school banned. They were Whittier's Ivy Leaguers. "Sure, the Franklins were the haves and we were the have-nots," Nixon told an interviewer in 1958, the first evidence of populism to emerge from Nixon's early days.

The Orthogonians "wanted to overthrow them," remembered one alumnus, "and the ferment was ripe and strong." The time was ready for revolt, and every account places young Nixon at the center of the action. He became the first Orthogonian president and also ensured his local political following.

He developed confidence in campus dramatics, even campaigning to bring dancing to the student body, which was one-fifth Quaker. He "sought applause as though it were a substitute for love," biographer Fawn Brodie wrote, "and the student vote fed this special hunger." She could have added that he was a contradiction from the start, emerging early on as the "enigma" critics of his presidency would regard him.

He was evidently split almost right down the middle between Hannah and Frank, behaving like one while wanting the world to believe that he was the other. From the Nixon side, he seems to have gotten his drive, intensity, and tempestuousness; certainly, his determination to beat the odds. From the Milhouses, and especially from Hannah herself, he seemed to have inherited the personal courtesies and often considerate behavior that sometimes astonished those who knew him only as the son of Frank Nixon.

His ability to win a tuition scholarship from the newly accredited but already competitive law school at Durham, North Carolina, aided by a strong recommendation from Whittier's president, Dr. William Dexter, brought him to Duke in 1934. He soon won respect for his seriousness of purpose. As a college librarian said, "He had to know people pretty well to let them see his frivolous side."

Thousands of pages of testimony by contemporaries testify to his skills, even from those who considered him a "grind," a "gloomy Gus." The young Nixon maintained the scholastic distinction he had achieved from early childhood, scoring high on his tests and serving on Duke's law review.

An additional financial bonus, which paid off in other ways as well, was an arrangement made by the dean, H. Claude Horack, for him to work on a special research problem in criminal law under the auspices of the National Youth Administration (NYA), a New Deal agency. Earning an extra thirty-five cents an hour as a student working for the NYA was not uncommon among his classmates, but the record suggests that even they recognized Nixon as especially hard pressed. He had every reason to be grateful. "I believe we've got the best darn law school in the country right at Duke," he wrote to Horack after becoming a member of the bar. "The atmosphere between students and faculty, the small size of student body, and the progressive attitude of the faculty convince me of that fact." He finished third in his class of Duke Law '37.

Unfortunate timing marked Nixon's entry into the job market. The economy, still suffering from the Great Depression, weakened in 1937 as the Roosevelt administration in Washington shied away from possible inflationary spending. Nixon's applications with New York City law firms were rejected. More disappointing, and certainly regarded by him as a personal rejection, was his failure to hook on with the Federal Bureau of Investigation, despite a boost from Dean Horack. Only many years later did he learn that he was never actually rejected; his application, tentatively accepted, was deferred until he passed the bar. Despite his admittance to the California bar on November 9, 1947, no verdict was actually delivered. The delay may well have led to giving the job as special agent to someone else. Whether that was what happened or, as Director J. Edgar Hoover later told him, he was the victim of budget cuts, such early failures were part of "the many self-perceived disappointments and humiliations Nixon confronted," and he "remained a cold and shy young man who could not make friends easily . . ."

He really had no choice but to return to Whittier, its population of 25,000 increasingly becoming part of the suburban Los Angeles sprawl. Straitlaced and provincial, that center of Southern California Quakerism was a larger version of Yorba Linda. It even fancied itself, in the words of one writer, as "a little gem of democracy," tolerant of its few blacks and Mexicans, no more class conscious than other communities of similar size and, as elsewhere, a place where success often depended on personal and family connections. He renewed his childhood association with the East Whittier Friends Church, where he had a born-again experience in 1926. Hannah has been quoted as calling her son "an intensely religious man," whose heritage also made for some characteristic stubbornness, although religion was never a very public part of his makeup. Equally important for his credentials in Whittier was his identification as a Republican, a choice he made official by registering to vote as a member of that party on June 15, 1938.

Grandfather Milhous helped place him with the local law firm of Wingert and Bewley, Whittier's oldest—not, perhaps, what might have been expected after his distinguished record at Duke, but gainful, nevertheless.

After opening an office in nearby La Habra, in 1939 he became a partner in the Wingert firm, newly named Wingert, Bewley, and Nixon. As with many young lawyers, especially the politically ambitious, he joined just about every civic association of businessmen and young attorneys. He moved on to become a member of the Whittier College board of trustees, its youngest board member ever, and headed the alumni association. He also served as assistant city attorney for Whittier. Prominent among those of importance in that phase of Nixon's career were such people as attorney Tom Bewley, Kyle Palmer, the editor of the *Los Angeles Times*, and Whittier banker Herman Perry.

In 1940, two years after Nixon's registration as a Republican, he made speeches for presidential candidate Wendell Willkie, then opposing FDR's third-term bid. Ola Florence, interviewed in 1986, had no trouble recalling his politics. "As far as I can remember him, he was always conservative. We did argue a lot. I absolutely adored President Roosevelt. I don't know why we were political. We kind of were and tended to argue over that," she said.

In that period, between Duke and Pearl Harbor, marriage followed, not to Ola, but to someone who resembled her. Brought together with Thelma Catherine Ryan (called Pat), when they were both in local theater in 1938, Nixon was decisive about the attractions of the amateur actress. An oft-told story recalls how he began his courtship by driving her to dates and then seeing to it that she got home all right.

Clearly intelligent and hard working, she had already lived much of what Nixon liked to regard as the "real world," a variety of part-time jobs including work as a radiologist's assistant in a Bronx hospital, and going on to earn a degree in merchandising from the University of Southern California, graduating *cum laude*. Pat, who was ten months older than he, was also tall, slender, serious, and reserved. She was rather startled early on when he informed her that, "Someday I'm going to marry you." They took their vows in a Quaker ceremony in the Mission Inn in Riverside on June 21, 1940. She went to work teaching business education in Whittier High School.

The Japanese attack of December 7, 1941, changed almost everyone's world. Weary of legal routines and eager to respond without upsetting his pacifist mother and other Milhouses, Nixon welcomed a suggestion that seems to have originated with a Duke professor, David Cavers. Cavers held a high-ranking position with the Office of Price Administration (OPA), one of the New Deal "alphabet" agencies. Nixon seized the chance "to go to Washington and observe the working of the government first-hand."

He saw another world, another culture, in the wartime capital. He served that office as a junior attorney in the tire-rationing section with sufficient competence to win promotion during his eight-month stint, but his memory of working in a branch of the New Deal bureaucracy in the capital confirmed his distaste for Washington life. He found himself in a world of liberal Democrats. The office's assumptions about rationing and price controls, especially in wartime, gave the Californian a negative taste of government bureaucracy. Too often, he thought, their thrust relied on government and tended to be antibusiness, which was especially true of the head of Nixon's section, Thomas Emerson, whose subsequent career at Yale Law School and activism included both the National Lawyers Guild and Henry Wallace's Progressive Party presidential campaign of 1948. Whatever touch of liberalism Nixon may have imbibed during his Duke years certainly had been diluted by the Rotarian world of Whittier and vanished altogether in Washington.

Nixon's immediate supervisor at the OPA, Thomas E. Harris, later recalled him as "hard-working and diligent," but, as quoted by biographer Stephen Ambrose, he was "uncomfortable among the liberals, the Eastern law-school graduates, the Jews he rubbed shoulders with on the job. No one thought of him as a right-winger in those days, but in style if not in politics he was thought of as a conservative." Nixon himself remarked later that some of those colleagues became "obsessed with their own power and seemed to delight in kicking people around, especially in the private sector." His lesson, he also explained, was that he "thought it was possible for government to do more than I later found it was practical to do."

At his first chance, he put aside family considerations and responded to the Navy's call for lawyers. "The problem with Quaker pacifism," Nixon later wrote, "it seemed to me, was that it could only work if one were fighting a civilized, compassionate enemy. In the face of Hitler and Tojo, pacifism not only failed to stop violence—it actually played into the hands of a barbarous foe and weakened home-front morale." Nixon was a young, able man with visions of a postwar political future. His OPA job could probably have given him a deferment, at least temporarily. His decision was simplified by the fact that he needed to take part in the war for any future political career. Early post–Pearl Harbor America would scorn pacifists and draft dodgers.

His years in service, between ages twenty-nine and thirty-three, were years of growth that removed him far from Whittier, geographically and culturally. They also clearly advanced his maturation in unexpected ways and boosted his future career beyond what his boyhood and student days had made possible.

The uniformed Nixon was commissioned as a lieutenant after two months at Officers' Candidate School at Quonset Point, Rhode Island, and then went on to a base in Ottumwa, Iowa. Pat had gone on working with the OPA in Washington but left the capital and joined him in Ottumwa, living up to her belief that "a woman must first and foremost be a homemaker," but she was ultimately forced to remain in the San Francisco Bay Area when Dick shipped out to join the South Pacific Combat Air Transport Command (SCAT) on the remote island of New Caledonia. Pat first got a job with the Office of Civilian Defense in San Francisco, then became an OPA secretary there and advanced to the position of price economist, so her monthly salary increased from $180 to $280. Nixon, meanwhile, found his new calling with the enlisted men in the South Pacific.

In a military that merged those of all backgrounds, especially during the years of selective service such as World War II and for much of the subsequent Cold War, democratizing social experiences were not unusual. For Richard Nixon, holder of not only an undergraduate degree, then not all that common, but also a law degree from Duke, life with his SCAT unit in the South Pacific was an enlightening experience. There can be little doubt that it did more than merely promote his self-confidence, but, unlike what he had known as a child and even in his recent milieu at Whittier, he found himself in a leadership position. The enlisted men in the Solomon Islands clearly responded to the officer they came to know as "Nick." Life with them was a reminder that he shared most of their working-class experiences and attitudes. They understood each other.

But it went beyond that, to those who shared his military rank. As one junior officer who served with him has been quoted, "He made an awful lot of sense. He had no more rank than most of us, he was our age generally speaking, but he commanded a lot of respect from the guys with whom he came in contact. When things got a bit hectic, he never lost his head. No matter how badly things got fouled up, Dick got his part of the operation straightened out and did it without a lot of hullabaloo."

He impressed his buddies, gaining their respect as a sharp poker player. The card game, which he had learned to play while still in civilian life, was a welcome antidote to a life where the absence of danger usually constituted boredom and loneliness. The young officer rose to what has been described as "a test of will and nerve," dealing the stakes and somewhat instinctively knowing just when to make his move. He seemed to seldom lose. "There are a hundred Navy officers who will tell you that Nick never lost a cent at poker," recalled one of the players. "He wasn't afraid of running a bluff," said another. "Sometimes the stakes were pretty big, but Nick had daring and had a flair for knowing what to do." He mastered the art of the "poker face" and came away with winnings that were later useful to help launch a political career. Nixon, while conceding that he "won a substantial pot," sounded a note of modesty when, much later, he wrote his memoirs. "My poker playing during this time has been somewhat exaggerated in terms of both my skill and my winning." He did take home nearly $8,000 from poker, a princely sum in those days.

Enlisted men were more likely to remember him as the "proprietor" of Nick's Hamburger Stand. He became adept at wheedling supplies from better stocked outfits and dispensing such prized luxuries as beer, hamburgers, and whiskey, while bartering "everything from captured Japanese rifles to introductions to the Army nurses who arrived to take care of the casualties."

By the time Japan was defeated, he left the Navy as Lieutenant Commander Nixon. At Bougainville in the Solomon Islands, his unit came under bombardment from Japanese planes. He also witnessed a horrific crash aboard an aircraft carrier. Left with no personal damage other than searing memories of conflict, he salvaged from the war the sobriquet of "Fighting Quaker," which came in handy after he responded to the following letter from Herman Perry, then manager of the Whittier branch of the Bank of America.

Dear Dick:

I am writing you this short note to ask if you would like to be a candidate for Congress on the Republican ticket in 1946.

Jerry Voorhis expects to run—registration is about 50-50. The Republicans are gaining.

Please airmail me your reply if you are interested.

Yours very truly,
H. L. Perry

2

From Whittier to Washington

The invitation to run for Congress reached Nixon while he was still in the Navy, awaiting his military discharge. He had agreed to complete the assignment as a Bureau of Aeronautics contracting officer and did not assume that he "should walk out in the middle of negotiations"; by 1946, he would be ready and willing to get back to California. He was enthusiastic about getting the call and Perry noted his excitement. It was a "wonderful surprise to learn that I was even being considered for the chance to run against Jerry Voorhis," Nixon told him.

Perry was eager to have Nixon. He and Pat had prepared themselves financially for the possibility, thanks to those poker winnings and recent savings, and Nixon left no doubt about his enthusiasm for fighting and winning. His would be an "aggressive, vigorous campaign on a platform of *practical* liberalism" that would become the "antidote the people have been looking for to take the place of Voorhis's particular brand of New Deal liberalism."

Voorhis's misfortune was that he was not up to making a strong defense on that level. If anything, remembered a fellow Democrat and later California governor, Pat Brown, he was very much the gentleman, "almost effeminate," a reformer, an aristocrat in politics. He has been called a visionary, an idealist, one whose views were shaped more by religion than by class and a sucker for populist impulses. Nixon would demonstrate that America, and certainly the citizens of California's Twelfth Congressional District, could not risk putting up with a man like Voorhis. If that took "rough-and-tumble politics," so be it.

Nixon's outlook was in tune with what was happening throughout the country. In those post-war months, the nation faced its first mid-term elections of the new era. Many prominent citizens of California's Twelfth, including bankers like Herman Perry and a variety of small businessmen and Republican activists, eagerly delighted in a newfound political activism. For them, it was not too soon to rid government of New Deal leftovers with their affinity for "socialism," even "communism"—all with, as Nixon had confirmed for himself, a passion for stifling regulatory strangulation of private enterprise. Nixon's early boosters were lawyers, realtors, insurance men, automobile dealers, mostly affluent Rotarian types, certainly comfortably middle class but not necessarily wealthy. Perry was not the only banker, but they were all friends of the man known in Whittier as Uncle Herman, the local "Mr. Republican." His small-town prominence was very much part of the culture represented by the chamber of commerce and political pros. His expressions about the "public interest" resounded with such phrases as "sound moral principles," "sound fiscal policies," and "one hundred percent American principles." Unable to keep the Democrats from coming to power in the first place, Perry was among those for whom the New Deal was unfortunate, and he had the good sense to oppose FDR. He was also, according to another friend of the campaign, "the political godfather of young Nixon." "Dick grew up under his wing," said Wallace Black. "He'd seen Dick grow up as a small boy in this town, and as a young man."

What else could Nixon want? He had the issues, the press, the political climate, and the momentum. The Voorhis dilemma is best illustrated by the following excerpt from an editorial that appeared in two of the district's papers: "*Jerry is not a Communist* but not many members of the House have voted against more measures the Communists vigorously oppose than he. It takes a smart politician to get the support of the CIO Political Action Committee in Washington and appeal to the voters at home as a conservative."

That winning campaign in 1946 made Richard Nixon a United States congressman. It also made him, in the view of those who were shocked by the reality that it was possible to unseat a Jerry Voorhis, one of the first significant GOP targets to emerge from the very early days of the Cold War. Nixon's vigorous challenge not only introduced him to the world of American politics but also helped to delineate the stormy rebelliousness that broke out against the New Deal once the fighting had come to an end. Communism itself, an issue that was only very tangential in Nixon's early political rhetoric, quite naturally drew charges of Democratic "statism" to a new level, especially with the compounding of difficulties with the Soviet Union during those early years after the war. Roosevelt's alleged "sell-out" at the Yalta Conference seemed to confirm the suspicions about the man who had been a four-term president until his death on April 12, 1945.

That 1946 campaign not only was Nixon's debut on the American political scene, but it created the imagery that marked his entire political career. In California's bipartisan political system of that time, his circulars showed him as a candidate deserving of wide, across-the-board support. He "knows what it means to earn a dollar—the problems of the working man." He wanted to go forward, not backward, from the New Deal, to make government work better than it could "with the governmental procedures and practices of yesterday." His call for "a sound progressive program in which government will work with and through private enterprise toward our goal of assuring housing, clothing, food, education and opportunity for every American" struck many postwar Americans as long due. Amid the chaos of conversion from wartime back to a peacetime footing, the Truman administration seemed flummoxed, especially during those months after Roosevelt's death. Nationally, Republicans campaigned under a slogan that asked, "Had Enough?"

When the Twelfth held its primaries, there were no surprises. Voorhis and Nixon had no trouble getting nominated. Voorhis got 7,000 more votes overall than Nixon, but that was less comfort for the Democratic incumbent than it might appear. His actual share of the total primary vote was down by 6.5 percent from the 1944 level. Still, he *was* the congressman, and he had the votes; Nixon was the neophyte with the burden of demonstrating that he could win.

On September 12, the developing international situation centering on Soviet intransigence, especially concerning their continued presence in Eastern Europe, took a new turn at home in a foreign policy speech by President Truman's secretary of commerce, Henry A. Wallace, that undoubtedly helped to ratchet up the political debate. Wallace, an FDR holdover who had served as vice president and was increasingly a maverick, placed the new administration on the defensive. His remarks to followers in New York's Madison Square Garden, an event tied to the labor-affiliated National Citizens Political Action Committee (NCPAC), castigated the United States for meddling with the sphere of Soviet influence and urged both nations to settle their differences.

Nixon turned up his pitch with the help of a new political consultant, one reputed to be an effective "gutter fighter," Murray Chotiner. In tones reminiscent of Chotiner's influence, Nixon charged that there "are those walking in high official places in our country who would destroy our constitutional principles through socialization of American free institutions. . . . These are the people who would lead us into a disastrous foreign policy whereby we will be guilty of collusion with other nations in depriving the people of smaller nations the very freedoms guaranteed by our Constitution."

Chotiner's elevation was the result of a string of victories for Republican candidates in California. He was noted for masterminding Earl Warren's gubernatorial campaign, in addition to his work for Senator William Knowland. If any lieutenant was able to push Nixon aside and run the show, it was Chotiner, whose stated prime objective of a successful campaign was, "Destroy your opponent."

The Nixon-Chotiner name association would became a staple of American politics. Nixon was a "fundamentally decent man," Garry Wills wrote, "until he took up politics and learned too well the lessons of a Murray Chotiner." He was present in one way or another in every Nixon fight but the last. We may never know who originated the anonymous phone calls that schemed to embarrass Voorhis. Was it Chotiner?

Within the context of such events, it remains puzzling that Voorhis was so surprisingly passive, unprepared for a fight. With the formal opening at his campaign came the Nixon argument that it was time "to clean house in Washington." He also charged that Voorhis's crowd constituted the same "left-wing group" that had taken over the state's Democratic Party. Nixon, sharpening his point, added at a late August rally in Whittier that he welcomed "the opposition of the PAC, with its Communist principles and huge slush fund." On Labor Day, in Whittier, he proudly accepted the "challenge of the PAC." With all that time to defend himself, Voorhis still failed to do his basic homework and was unprepared for the obvious response to this challenge.

The decisive showdown took place at South Pasadena High School. On the stage that evening, Voorhis was left blank, utterly on the defensive, upholding a position where he was "almost forced to defend the New Deal," as one observer described the scene in that conservative community. The event, exciting for a small town in that pre-television era, featured not "mud-slinging," according to witnesses, but "just straight-from-the-shoulder debating."

Voorhis himself had initiated the challenge to defend himself from taints of radicalism that were enhanced because of his endorsement by NCPAC. He naively demanded "proof" that Nixon had the goods. Nixon, in turn, played political theater by dramatically thrusting a mimeographed NCPAC recommendation in front of his opponent's face. "Voorhis was completely taken by surprise," one of his aides conceded. He was left flat-footed, unable to explain the differences between the union itself and its political arm, the NCPAC, from its local CIO-PAC chapter. Nixon sealed his point by offering enough evidence to show that distinctions were purely technical. Voorhis "fumbled and was flustered."

Voorhis never recovered from doubts about his loyalty. "If some of my rhetoric seems overstated now," Nixon later wrote, "it was nonetheless in keeping with the approach that seasoned Republican politicians were using that year."

Nixon had a self-serving justification for his blistering rhetoric: Everybody was doing it. Far from having been a non-issue, as some of Nixon's detractors would later claim, the matter of communism virtually submerged everything else Nixon was saying. Right from the start, he visualized an America that was dedicated to making the world free for capitalism. Nor did he deny, as did the counterreformers, that social service responsibilities must come with laissez-faire government. Nixon called for a federal government that served as a guardian, not a regulator. He was talking to a nation for whom FDR "was virtually a god," and, as an early acquaintance pointed out, Nixon, like that god, had the capacity to arouse "very bitter hatred and animosity." In words anathema to that generation of New Deal–oriented commentators, Nixon labeled a "controlled economy . . . a failure" and hailed President Truman's "belated lifting of price controls on meat." A Republican congress would solve the crisis brought about by the shortage of meat and housing. He called for legislation to outlaw jurisdictional strikes and for transferring rent controls to state and local governments, where they should be administered at "equitable" levels. A typical talking point, especially in pursuit of the veterans' vote, was that "America can best fulfill its obligation to the GI by maintaining a form of economic government where an opportunity is given him to do his job. The secret of American success and hope for the future is to give the GI a government that allows him to perform the kind of job he has determined to do without restricting him by regimentation."

Nixon also spoke out for racial justice. "Let us always remember," he said, "that we in America live under a form of government which recognizes that all men are born free and equal," he said at the East Whittier Friends Church. Then, reciting the names of three nationally known bigots, he called them "just as dangerous to the preservation of the American way of life on the one hand as are the Communists on the other." Nixon's rhetoric was usually well-targeted, sharp, and provocative.

Nixon, as a conservative Republican, would have been elected in any event. William Knowland, a fellow rightist, was returned to the Senate with 55 percent of the vote against Will Rogers, Jr., and Earl Warren, favored by

Democrats as well as the GOP, won a second term as governor. Statewide, the Republican Party gained ten congressional seats. Such realities aside, that first Nixon election and the unfolding of his subsequent career marked that victory as notable and controversial long afterward.

* * *

One is hard pressed to consider the rise of Richard Nixon without thinking about John F. Kennedy, another ambitious young man who had served in the South Pacific during World War II and ventured into political careers immediately afterward. To Richard Nixon, sworn in with Kennedy at the opening of the Eightieth Congress, their polar relationships could hardly have been more vivid or more galling. Kennedy, unlike Nixon, derived his political power from the liberal and working-class constituency in Massachusetts, still very Irish and still very Democratic, which was reflected in their respective views toward the National Labor Relations Act of 1947, popularly known as the Taft-Hartley bill.

The effort to limit the ability of unions to organize and bargain collectively was facing its first serious postwar challenge, fueled by a spate of significant walkouts that paralyzed some key industries. Unionists cited their need to update take-home pay because wartime restrictions on wages had caused them to fall behind; it wasn't fair to keep them down forever. Kennedy objected to what he called "repressive and vindictive labor legislation," but, at the same time, expressed doubts about labor's future if unions insisted "upon special privilege and unfair advantage." To the pro-labor cause, that smacked of having it both ways.

Nearly four decades later, speaking of Kennedy, Nixon recalled that "Neither of us was an extremist. Kennedy was not the favorite of the left of his party. . . . He opposed Taft-Hartley only for political purposes. We saw eye-to-eye on foreign policy—aid to Greece and Turkey, the Marshall Plan."

Nixon's freshman appointment to the Education and Labor Committee was a political plum, giving him a voice in the heated labor conflict. Although by the time of Taft-Hartley's enactment, the spate of walkouts had basically cooled off, large segments of the public, encouraged by representatives of management, were convinced that the New Deal had obligated itself too deeply to "big labor." The "imbalance" needed to be redressed.

An additional plum for Nixon was the Education and Labor Committee's series of hearings that spring that publicized how Communist-led local union leadership had acted contrary to the best interests of defense production. Nixon made headlines when Republican House Speaker Joe Martin appointed him to the highly desirable House Committee on Un-American Activities (HUAC). First under the chairmanship of Representative Martin Dies of Texas, the committee's hearings became an example of unseemly congressional behavior. Newspapers reported the undermining of the nation by sinister organizations and names. By 1947, when the HUAC hearings took place, three-fifths of the public agreed that Communists were loyal to a dangerous foreign power and that such membership should be outlawed.

That fall, in an investigation into Communist influences in the motion picture industry, insinuations and spurious charges were floated before the public recklessly. Nixon's own dissent from some of the HUAC style emerged during the testimony of producer Jack L. Warner, who had made a wartime film called *Mission to Moscow*, but it did not spare him from association with its excesses. The committee was stacked, Nixon later agreed; it was a gaggle of primitives, "habitually unfair," widely condemned by liberals. He was also, as a review of the proceedings confirmed, its most articulate member.

Nixon's association helped to establish his political career, but it also haunted his reputation in "reputable" political circles. Later publicity about the ilk of those colleagues on that committee, especially the blatant racism of such members as Mississippi's John Rankin, were bad enough. In a political environment that had much of the liberal media still on the alert for anti-Communist "yahoos" engaged in Red-hunting, Nixon's role with HUAC was a relatively minor long-term stain on his record.

More damning, certainly in the eyes of those unforgiving for his defeat of Voorhis, was his authorship of the Mundt-Nixon bill, which originated in that committee. Rather than trying to outlaw the American Communist Party, as Thomas and others had wanted, Nixon joined with Senator Karl Mundt of South Dakota to sponsor a bill requiring the annual registration of Communist organizations and their members. After clearing the House in a 319 to 58 roll call vote, the legislation, formally known as the Subversive Activities Control Bill, languished in the Senate.

The bill was the only piece of legislation that ever bore Nixon's name. Even FBI Director J. Edgar Hoover, no civil libertarian, cautioned about driving suspects underground and creating martyrdom. In the long run, other than carrying the Nixon name and marking a step in the process of responding to the growing fear of internal subversion, that matter of doubtful loyalty became the basis for the more significant Communist Control Act of 1950.

The issue also validated Nixon's 1948 fight for a second congressional term. Sharply opposed by his rival, for "one of the most dangerous measures ever to come before Congress" and its promise of "guilt by association," Nixon nevertheless prevailed and won handily, 21,411 votes to 16,808.

Another boost during those years, when his tactics in beating Voorhis and his HUAC membership were mostly what outsiders heard about him, was his appointment by

Speaker Martin to what came to be called the Herter Committee. More formally, a Select Committee on Foreign Aid, it was a 19-member congressional contingent to travel to Europe in an effort to assess appropriate non-military programs to strengthen the continent's resistance to Moscow. Nixon's inclusion was not only a matter of political balance, since he was a Westerner and the youngest member of the group, but it also recognized his emergence as the supporter of a bipartisan foreign policy consensus behind Truman. Nixon, who had dabbled with foreign policy while at Duke, lacked experience in such matters. But his association with the committee, which included extensive travels throughout Europe, confirmed his internationalism.

It is fair to say, as historian Irwin Gellman pointed out, that "What made Nixon unique was his ability to articulate two apparently dissimilar themes: internationalism and anticommunism." He followed through with his support of the Marshall Plan and its heavy spending to aid Western European recovery in that valiant effort to prop it up economically against Russian expansionist tendencies. He also voted with the Democratic majority on military aid to Greece and Turkey, the major administration's response to the perceived Soviet threat to the Middle East. It was also a blow to what remained of Republican isolationism. He returned to the Twelfth to explore and support those positions in defiance of those local traditionalists still wedded to "America first," always careful to explain why giving foreign aid to Europe truly was in the nation's best interest.

* * *

In that freshman year, and in a period that spanned his re-election activities at home, Nixon emerged as the premier player in the drama that involved Alger Hiss. Not until July 31, 1948, did the matter even fall into HUAC's provenance. One Elizabeth Bentley, the "Red spy queen" of the affair, faced the committee to tell her story. Her deceased boyfriend had served as a courier of secret documents (along with Bentley herself, who had been paid at least $2,000) that were funneled to Soviet spies. Just a few days later, the HUAC chairman, Parnell Thomas, introduced one who became a key player, another ex-Communist and now a journalist, Whittaker Chambers. It was Chambers who, on August 3, contributed another bombshell, the activities of brothers Donald and Alger Hiss as members of a Red cell in Washington. Alger, of course, took the spotlight. He had served in various capacities in the State Department and, most interesting for those still out to dub Roosevelt as a man "who gave away the shop" to the Soviets, was his service as an adviser to FDR at the Yalta Conference. Chambers told the committee about his own resignation from the Communist Party, but said that Hiss had refused to do so at his urging in 1937.

Nixon emerged as the HUAC member best positioned and perceptive to pursue the point. He found the accused one among "a considerable number of perfectly loyal citizens whose theaters of operation are the nation's mass media and universities, its scholarly foundations, and its government bureaucracies" who advance by pedigree and glamour and deceive the world with cultivated facades, as he later wrote in *Six Crises*.

Contrast that style, as Nixon quickly did, with Chambers, the rumpled Mr. Everyman. Eager to follow through by questioning Chambers further in executive session, he confronted him before a special three-member subcommittee in New York's federal courthouse. He heard personal details about Hiss that could only have come from an intimate acquaintance. On August 25, at HUAC's final session, Hiss appeared and challenged Chambers to go public with his allegations without the cover of congressional immunity. Chambers did just that, during the course of a "Meet the Press" radio interview with the flat statement that "Alger Hiss was a Communist and may still be one." Chambers went from there to recover government documents hidden in the Brooklyn apartment house of his wife's nephew. The cache consisted of both handwritten and typewritten papers, some recorded on microfilm. He placed the microfilm in a hollowed-out pumpkin, safeguarding the material, presumably, from hostile Justice Department investigators eager to uphold the sanitization of the New Deal.

Nixon and his investigators followed through. When a grand jury was impaneled (after Nixon had been safely re-elected), Hiss was indicted. Two trials followed, the first ending in a hung jury, and the second with a conviction on two counts of perjury (as the statute of limitations for espionage had expired). Hiss was sentenced to spend five years at the federal penitentiary at Lewisburg, Pennsylvania, for having lied about his acquaintance with Chambers and his membership in the Communist Party.

Nixon had been instrumental in convincing Americans of the gravity of potential enemy infiltration. At that relatively early stage of what became known to historians as the "second Red Scare" (the first having been the period following World War I, where a central role was played by Attorney General Archibald Palmer), the affair involving the New Deal foreign policy adviser, Hiss, was the most dramatic confirmation that there were, indeed, leaks in the New Deal's internal security apparatus (if it could even be dignified by that description), which, to view it most charitably, certainly was lax.

Nixon's triumph also helped prepare the way for Joe McCarthy, whose dramatic charge that 205 Communists worked for the State Department was made on February 9, 1950, just two weeks after Nixon's review of the case before the House of Representatives. It won him fame and certainly helped him advance to the vice presidency. Redbaiting, as historian David Greenberg has pointed out, "was just one element of a more fully rounded identity as a heroic American everyman." It should be understandable, then, to note how quickly the whole thing moved from initial revelations to follow-up hearings to convictions.

The Hiss case established Nixon as a controversial figure. Nixon had exposed a true-blue New Dealer; administration loyalists had made an icon openly abused by die-hard reactionaries, embittered for the rest of his life by having been portrayed as a villain for having acted in the best interest of national security. He thought that journalists, in contemporary analyses and in magazine articles long afterward, contributed to the creation of Richard Nixon as a dark, insidious character, a view of the press that reflected more anger than reality. He remained convinced that only a few good journalists could be trusted to get a story straight, and they were usually along with the brainwashed little professors in elite schools, who had forgotten that their real purpose was education, not liberal indoctrination. There were examples galore in 1946, and what was true of '46 was doubly so in '50 when Helen Gahagan Douglas opposed him for the Senate. That anomaly was especially vivid when he defeated her in a celebrated race that virtually followed on the heels of the Hiss case.

Perception, it is often said, is more important than reality. What came out of that campaign for the Senate in 1950, other than his victory over Congresswoman Douglas, was a set of impressions that fed the wariness about his tenacity, or even ruthlessness, in mounting a counterattack to the world of the New Deal. For the rest of his career, the negative aura that hung around Nixon included recollections about "what he did to Helen."

To Nixon, Douglas, who was first elected to the House of Representatives in 1944, epitomized the mushiness of liberal politics. Her public service included a heritage that combined both the New Deal and the so-called "popular front" with its romantic memories of the Soviet and American wartime collaboration together with the belief that it could continue to serve the cause of world peace in a post-Nazi world. More moderate in recent years, as Soviet villainy became clearer, she nevertheless remained well to the left and with dubious associations. The *Los Angeles Times* confirmed suspicions of the congresswoman when it termed her a "glamorous actress who, though not a Communist, voted the Communist party line in Congress innumerable times, and was the darling of the Hollywood parlor pinks and Reds." She also was the only member of the state's congressional delegation to oppose returning control of the offshore tidelands oil back to the states from the federal government, an outrage in a state where the tidelands question was pivotal. Willingness to continue federal control over such richness was virtually a litmus test of liberalism. Wresting it from Washington meant returning decisions to the much more favorable, controllable, and accessible statehouse in Sacramento. How could Douglas say she represented California's interests?

The former actress was, in addition, married to a well-known movie star, Melvyn Douglas, also a political activist and a West Coast leader of Americans for Democratic Action, anti-communist but generically a New Deal liberal.

For California politics with its fluid party lines, Douglas, like Voorhis before her, was the maverick. Nixon was the orthodox conservative. In those primaries, the Democratic challenger, Manchester Boddy, took the initiative by attacking Douglas for softness toward communism and hit hard at her opposition to Truman's call for aid to Greece and Turkey.

Nixon, nevertheless, concluded that whatever Democratic incumbent Senator Sheridan Downey's attractions, the moment had come for his own effort. As he wrote to a leading supporter on August 11, 1949, he had "such an unusual opportunity that the risk is worth taking." The analysis was consistent with the realpolitik understanding of power that characterized his entire political career. Simply put, the Hiss case had made him "hot," and it was the time to strike, even if giving up his House seat meant forfeiting the perks of seniority. There was, he concluded, the chance that splitting the opposition, which could result in a Douglas candidacy, would clear the way. Support was not hard to find, including from some of the state's leading papers and its Republican senator, William Knowland. So Nixon agreed to run for the Senate with the promise that it would be "simply the choice between freedom and state socialism." Later, Downey pleaded ill health and dropped out of the Democratic primary. His replacement was *Los Angeles Daily News* publisher Manchester Boddy. Shrewdly, Nixon then determined to unite Republicans and Democrats by making Douglas symbolic of what had gone wrong in Washington.

That strategy was preempted when Downey, having stepped aside, then backed Boddy. Boddy attacked Douglas by citing her as "evidence of a statewide conspiracy on the part of this small subversive clique of red-hots to capture, through stealth and cunning, the nerve centers of our Democratic party." A Boddy campaign sheet proclaimed that "There's no such thing as being a 'little communistic' or a 'little socialistic.'" It also announced, in bright red letters, that the "Record Shows Rep. Douglas Voted With Extreme Radicals." It was also through a Boddy flyer that Douglas was first linked with the voting record of New York City's left-wing congressman, Vito Marcantonio. Boddy even repeatedly advanced the charge that, "on four previous occasions, Mrs. Douglas and Marcantonio voted in the same way against similar bills to support the investigation of Communists, Fascists and the Ku Klux Klan. On April 28, 1950, Boddy's paper, *Democratic News*, dismissed Douglas as the "pink lady," thereby coining one of the more memorable terms of the campaign, one almost always attributed to Nixon. Reminiscent of the 1946 campaign, too many anonymous phone calls were received by too many people, each warning voters about Douglas's associations.

Nixon himself was smeared by becoming identified as the candidate of a noted anti-Semite, Gerald L. K. Smith, who headed the Christian Nationalist Crusade. Smith pleaded to "help Richard Nixon get rid of the Jew-Communists," which, of course, in his mind, included Douglas, whose husband was of half-Jewish origin. Nixon spurned Smith, denouncing "anti-Semitism in whatever form it appears." He also accepted the endorsement of the Anti-Defamation League (ADL), which praised his record as "clear on the question of the hate mongers" and for being "quick to repudiate all such bigots." Nixon also dismissed allegations of anti-Semitism by reminding voters that his campaign manager and "close friend" Murray Chotiner was Jewish.

The final month of the campaign was fought "almost like a holy crusade," with each side simply trying to gain an advantage over concern with the "rational basis of the issues"—in other words, do or die campaigning. While refusing to debate Nixon, Douglas charged a Nixon-Marcantonio voting comparison in a circular that said, "You pick the Congressman the Kremlin loves!" and claimed that, while he "cries Communist," he "voted consistently in agreement" with Marcantonio's pro-Communist position on Korea. Her accusations shrewdly accused Nixon of budget cutting that weakened the American effort in Korea. She had simply distorted his votes. They were, in reality, consistent with his Republican colleagues' efforts to fully fund efforts to thwart Communist expansion throughout the Far East.

He came away an easy victor, elected to the U. S. Senate just four years after his political debut, just as he turned thirty-eight, and with 59.2 percent of the total vote—achieved in a state with a Democratic majority. Roman Catholics also continued to wean themselves away from the Democrats, a sure sign of the approaching Age of Nixon. A study by Stanford University's Institute of Journalistic

Studies, for example, revealed that Nixon was actually backed by newspapers with 1,322,895 readers, compared to the pro-Douglas readership of 265,397. Moreover, not a single one of Douglas's local papers had a Sunday edition. The region's dominant paper, the *Los Angeles Times*, devoted 59 percent of its coverage to material that complained about Douglas, contrasted with only five percent that was critical of Nixon.

As with his encounters with Voorhis and Hiss, the triumph was as costly as it was decisive. His critics, conceded a friendly early biographer, "never fail to observe that in 1950 he conducted a 'vicious smear campaign' against Helen Gahagan Douglas." His reputation was established: a reactionary anticommunist zealot, a tool of Murray Chotiner and "in bed" with Gerald L. K. Smith, willing to throw any falsehood and innuendo against an idealistic opponent, the quintessence of political immorality.

Richard Nixon, already established as one of the most controversial politicians in America, was thereafter burdened with the sin of ruthless politicking. That campaign, in fact, became embellished in memory as journalist after journalist, especially in the opinionated leftist magazines popular with liberals, piled up on the early image of Nixon as an ogre, leaving an image of a reactionary anticommunist zealot unsparing of falsehoods and innuendos.

Democrats, meanwhile, who sought comfort because the Republicans failed to win control of either house or to approximate the customary gains by the "out" party, minimized the significance of losing key New and Fair Deal stalwarts. It was quite enough for Republican conservatives to take full advantage of all the cumulative vulnerabilities of a party long in power. Whether irresponsible tactics could yield responsible government was another question. If he already was, to some, a shrewd and not especially savory political figure, his reputation would soon suffer even more.

3

You're My Boy

The image of "Tricky Dick" emerged during this time and became more deeply engrained as time went on. While still strongly influenced by the most liberal aspect of the New Deal, Americans were at a political watershed. More and more, Nixon began to represent the sinister face of the future. That became especially ominous with the intensifying Red hunt, spurred successively by the fall of Chiang Kai-shek in China, the flamboyant debut of Joe McCarthy's crusade as the savior of American freedom from the "Red menace," and, in June 1950, the North Korean invasion of the South across the thirty-eighth parallel.

Even before the name McCarthy became symbolic of a contentious time, Richard Nixon had become associated with what liberals feared was a deteriorating political climate. It was Nixon who was already identified with the powerful supporters of the Chiang Kai-shek government in Peking, known as the China lobby, the thrust of McCarthyism over Truman and the Democrats, and a new post–Cold War stridency in American foreign policy. Later, muckraking articles described his villainy vis-à-vis Voorhis and Douglas (helping to inspire a "poor Helen" myth), and a series by Philip Horton that tied him closely to the lobby.

While he may have made the most of opportunities to get a place on the political map, Nixon threw in his lot with Republican hard-liners of the early 1950s. His pitch was almost indistinguishable from those who took up such early Cold War issues as the "loss" of China and the almost simultaneous Soviet acquisition of an atomic bomb, which was detonated in 1949.

He lost no time in condemning the Truman administration right after the North Korean invasion of South Korea in June 1950. He took the Senate floor to blame Secretary of State Dean Acheson for making a United Nations speech that failed to draw the U.S. security line at the thirty-eighth parallel. Nothing, however, aroused him as much as when the president fired for insubordination the American commander in the Pacific, General Douglas MacArthur, on April 10, 1951. Nixon immediately threw in his support and fiery rhetoric, and went so far as to sponsor a Senate resolution that called for restoring the general to "the commands from which he was removed."

The president, Nixon argued, had removed the wrong man. He should have fired his secretary of state. Truman's move was "a gross insult to General MacArthur and to the American people." Nixon's office quickly received some 30,000 supportive letters and 6,000 telegrams. Nixon, encouraged by his constituents, including enthusiastic support from his Quaker friends in Whittier, subsequently reiterated that "ending the war" the MacArthur way, and with honor, was the way to go, even if it meant thrusting American power more deeply into the Korean peninsula and, if need be, across the Yalu River and into China itself. Fully embracing the MacArthur cause, he advocated the "unleashing" of Chiang from Formosa, a favorite battle cry of the Asia First people. Even going one step further, Nixon urged strategic bombing to destroy targets inside China and for the United Nations, which had originally endorsed Truman's response to the invasion, to leave the entire job up to the U.S. His foreign policy positions, so supportive of the Truman administration on European containment matters, and so opposed to the new Communist regime in China, had clearly come to endorse what the Taft-Knowland-MacArthur wing of the party had articulated as the dominant Republican line.

Nixon's voting record in both the House and Senate had attractions for both major Republican wings. Such eastern internationalists as New York's Governor Tom Dewey, the GOP's two-time losing presidential candidate, and Massachusetts Senator Henry Cabot Lodge, Jr., representative of the party's moderates, eyed a Californian who appreciated that the world was round.

More important than anything else, the leading presidential aspirant, Dwight D. Eisenhower, kept his eyes on the political importance of California. The state even had a Republican governor, Earl Warren, which insured that a kick upstairs for Nixon would lead to his replacement by another Republican rather than the loss of a vital Senate seat. The Eisenhower camp, daily more confident of beating out Taft, had basically arrived at its decision. Eisenhower himself was sold on the wisdom of going before the party with the man who seemed eager, competent, intelligent, and, as he told Nixon, had not only nabbed Hiss but had done so fairly. An Eisenhower-Nixon ticket confirmed that Republicans had passed a watershed. The GOP's majority had been forced to swallow realities. Winning was more important than living with Taft on love alone. Even many of those who wore "I Like Ike" buttons backed him less for ideological reasons than because he was their best hope.

The coming of an Eisenhower-Nixon ticket was visible in several ways long before the 1952 convention. No politician was closer to the draft-Ike movement than New

The GOP's new ticket, Ike and Dick, at Chicago's Blackstone Hotel on July 12, 1952 © Bettmann/Corbis

York's governor, and Nixon was Tom Dewey's choice that spring to appear as the main speaker at the state party's major fund-raiser at the Waldorf-Astoria. Once in Chicago at the convention, he joined with the Dewey forces over the matter of the criteria for certifying delegates, an issue that became essential for turning back the Taftites who carried the flag for the GOP's power in the nation's heartland. In league with Dewey and Lodge, Nixon denounced what he called "the Texas grab," which helped set back the Taft claims for a share of Georgia's delegation.

Not surprisingly, Nixon was suspected of engaging in the kind of maneuvering within his own delegation that "reinforced the view of a Nixon who was little more than a crafty, unprincipled tactician whose services were forever on the open market." He was seen as serving, in effect, as kind of a Trojan horse within a California delegation pledged by law to hold at least its first-ballot votes for favorite son Earl Warren. Once they were allowed to break away, enough of them could help to put Taft over the top.

Eisenhower's own nomination for the presidency came after the delegates closed ranks following the first ballot to make the choice unanimous. So confident was he that Nixon would become his running mate that he was able to give the appearance of "neutrality" by detaching himself from the battle and delegating the actual recommendation to friends and supporters led by Herbert Brownell, who chaired the session. During that process, which took less than two hours, Dewey described Nixon's attractions, including his youth and public speaking strengths. In effect, there was no contest: Nixon would be in the best position to bring balance and votes to the ticket. Eisenhower, appearing to the convention afterward, declared that he had been called "to lead a great crusade—for freedom in America and in the world." Nixon's acceptance speech promised "a fighting campaign."

The convention, noted one prominent observer, was a fight between the "Old Guard" and the "New Order." The problem of the latter, he wrote, was "whether it can also break the *tradition* of the Old Guard and, convince the electorate that it is broken. In brief, it must close the gap between the nominee and convention." Nixon, the sop to the former with the hope of electoral success, was there, as he explained in a 1984 interview, "only because of the Hiss case, but my record as an internationalist in foreign affairs and in domestic affairs didn't satisfy them."

* * *

Believers in "new" Nixons emerging from time to time will find some substance from accounts of what happened when he became the vice presidential candidate during

Eisenhower's campaign to return Republican control to the White House. Long absence from power, many "years in the wilderness" encourages desperation, precisely the Grand Old Party's barrier to overcome in 1952. In retrospect, a ticket headed by the most popular general to come out of World War II should have been a shoo-in, but few were willing to take that for granted, certainly not after the shocking loss of Tom Dewey to Truman only four years earlier. Eisenhower, moreover, seemed unskilled in partisan political ways, unprepared to tackle the kind of infighting demanded both by campaigning and holding elective office. Did he even know much about domestic matters? Conservative Republicans, especially, doubted whether he was equipped, as they certainly thought Robert Taft and others were, to turn the nation away from the "socialistic" New Deal "statism" imposed by liberal Democrats. It was, in short, time for change, for moving away from controls and high taxes and toward more reliance on free enterprise and individual initiative. Conservative Democrats, especially in the South, emphasized "states' rights," as had the 1948 rebellious third party headed by Strom Thurmond of South Carolina, the so-called Dixiecrats who fought under the banner of States' Rights Democrats.

More politically repulsive to the mass of voters, at least for the immediate future, was the kind of political corruption especially common to prolonged entrenchment in power. In retrospect, it seems like a more innocent time. Much was made of the kind of graft that involved payoffs that centered on such now seemingly trivial items as deep freezers and mink coats. Such were the scandalous doings of Democrats grown fat with power.

Foreign policy had also become a sore point, even containment itself. Nixon, in his brief senatorial career, had certainly reflected the Asia First unhappiness about Communist gains across the Pacific. More and more, however,

Cold War politics had begun to focus on vulnerabilities in Europe, including the very containment program for which history has given the Truman presidency such high marks. Almost forgotten is the unhappiness of many Americans, especially those of Eastern European origin, with continued Soviet occupation and absorption of their homelands. Those in America who had eased Moscow's way, if not actually "sold out" to the Communists, were not hard to find, starting with FDR's concessions to "Uncle Joe" Stalin at Yalta. Specifically targeting Eastern Europe, the Republican foreign policy plank promised to "liberate" and free the "captive peoples," campaign oratory that translated as "rolling back" Communism without explaining exactly how that would be done. Sensationalized headlines publicized revelations about fairly prominent and more obscure "subversives" accused of serving the Communist cause, both legally and illegally. Overwhelmingly their names were largely associated in one way or another with the Democrats. Alger Hiss, whose downfall was the most prominent Nixon achievement, had surely dramatized the insidiousness of their existence. Along came Senator Joseph R. McCarthy's dramatics in February 1950 that alleged that there actually were 205 Communists in the State Department.

Richard Nixon, for all the credit he received as an anti-Communist, was no Joe McCarthy. But along with most of those who thirsted for power at the time, he took the cue. He promised, at the outset of his vice presidential campaign, for example, to make "Communist subversion and corruption the theme of every speech from now until the election." And, with the sharp rhetorical flourishes that became characteristic of his power as a speaker, he added, "If the record itself smears, let it smear. If the dry rot of corruption and communism, which has eaten deep into our body politic during the past seven years, can only be chopped out with a hatchet—then let's call for a hatchet." In that political climate, the Democratic presidential candidate, Adlai E. Stevenson of Illinois, was an "apologist" because he had been a character witness for Alger Hiss. Stevenson, in one of Nixon's more memorable campaign lines, was "Adlai the appeaser . . . who got a Ph.D. degree from [Dean] Acheson's College of Cowardly containment." For Nixon, whose early congressional career had been distinguished by his support for the essentials of the containment policy, especially the Marshall Plan and the creation of the North Atlantic Treaty Organization (NATO), it was a sharp change of course. While the head of the ticket campaigned as an honorable competitor, his running mate played the "hatchet man" role, not only by trying to smother the administration and the Democrats under often not very subtle intimations of unwillingness to meet the communist challenge, but also for the scandals in Washington that unsettled the country.

A favorite theme, one that had become familiar, exaggerated his hardscrabble background. As biographer Stephen Ambrose has noted, he built up a self-portrait that "stressed the 'Poor Richard'" theme, which included taking liberties with the truth about Pat never having been on a federal payroll and how little they cared for material things. While it was true that making money was not the prime attraction for him as a politician, his self-portrait suggested that "he entered politics to slay dragons."

Yet as early as that period, and continuing until his eventual resignation as president, the Democrats saw him, in Ambrose's words, "as the dirtiest man in town, worse than McCarthy, a smear artist without parallel." That imagery was as inflated as some of his rhetoric, but the negative effect could never be shaken. Every questionable step became ample verification that he was the "most dangerous man in politics."

Eisenhower, the war hero general, was too innocent, too obviously more wholesome, above reproach. Nixon, however, had drawn enough contempt from his opponents to be easily the most vulnerable candidate on the Republican national ticket. So the campaign changed, and with it, Nixon's reputation, when the *New York Post*, then a crusading liberal paper that proudly tried to keep New Deal liberalism alive, let loose with charges that he had a "secret fund."

The publishers could hardly have timed their bomb better. Two months after the convention and less than two months before election day, the paper ran the following headline: "Secret Rich Men's Trust Fund Keeps Nixon in Style Beyond His Salary." Some 75 mostly familiar Nixon supporters had contributed to develop reserves for miscellaneous expenditures that went beyond the budgetary ceiling. (Adlai Stevenson, it was later revealed, had a larger fund.) Subsequent professional auditing confirmed that it was neither secret nor illegal.

But for the Republicans and Ike, after slamming Democratic scandals, it was downright embarrassing. Eisenhower acknowledged the hypocrisy of his own "crusade" if "we, ourselves, aren't as clean as a hound's tooth." Nixon later wrote that he felt "like the little boy caught with jam on his face."

Panicky Republicans feared another 1948 collapse. The man blamed by many as the architect of that disaster, Tom Dewey, told both Nixon and Eisenhower that the decision about whether to dump the senator should be made by "the American people." Almost 100 newspapers that weighed in on the subject nationally, most of them supporters of the Republican ticket, deplored the situation by two to one; some demanded immediate withdrawal. Eisenhower was typically discreet, reluctant to decide prematurely. He told a top aide that "if Nixon has to go, we cannot win." But, it was obvious, the ticket had to do *something*. How else could he demonstrate leadership? Nixon's campaign, meanwhile, ran into hostile crowds. Many called for his withdrawal.

At Marysville, California, he delayed his campaign train and told the crowd that all this had been expected. After his nomination, in fact, he had been warned that "if I continue to attack the Communists and the crooks in this government they would continue to smear me. Then, warming up to the responsive crowd, he added, "believe me, you can expect that they will continue to do so." Reminding them of his role in the Hiss case, he told them, "Ever since . . . the Communists, the left-wingers, have been fighting me with every smear that they have been able to do."

But he failed to get any clear-cut support from Eisenhower, who called to tell him that he agreed with Dewey's notion of leaving it up to the public by making a nationwide television speech. He did not want to be accused of "condoning wrongdoing." An exasperated Nixon, wanting to know just where Ike stood on the matter but, still left dangling, said into the phone, "General, a time comes in politics when you have to shit or get off the pot!" "Keep your chin up" was all Ike could say as he broke off their little talk.

Nixon interrupted his campaign and flew with Pat from Portland to Los Angeles to prepare his remarks. With financial arrangements already made and actual delivery before the camera planned for the El Capitan Theater in Hollywood, Nixon heard from Dewey, who told him that the general's "top advisers" thought that he had to step down. The talk should go on, said New York's governor, but the sacrifice had to be made so that he would not risk endangering the rest of the ticket.

The "Checkers speech," as it soon became known, was one of the earliest, and perhaps most heralded, political events in the early history of television. The speech on the evening of September 23 was not memorized in what became the more familiar style; it was carefully outlined and artfully staged. The leading roles were, after all, being played by Richard Nixon, a veteran of amateur theatrics, and Pat Ryan Nixon, a fellow thespian from Whittier days. She sat next to him as he spoke, the camera recording her tense but confident and admiring expression. She was as much of a prop as the American flag.

Nixon began by acknowledging that it would have been morally wrong if the money had gone for his personal use. But that was not the case: "Not one cent . . . ever went to my personal use. Every penny of it was used to pay for political expenses that I did not think should be charged to the taxpayers of the United States." He cited the reports from his lawyers and accountants, quoting their exonerating words.

That left him with the problems reminiscent of Jefferson Smith, the idyllic hero of Frank Capra's popular 1939 movie, *Mr. Smith Goes to Washington*: merely driving a 1950 Oldsmobile, $3,000 in equity in a California house being occupied by his parents, $20,000 in his Washington property, and just $4,000 in life insurance, plus a GI term policy due to expire in two years. Other than that, he had "no stocks or bonds; no interest in any other property or business." He had $38,500 in debts, mostly represented by mortgages on his two houses. "That's what we have," he told his vast radio and television audience. "And that's what we owe. It isn't very much. But Pat and I have the satisfaction that every dime that we have got is honestly ours." Almost as an afterthought, he said what he had told crowds in the West, "I should say this, that Pat doesn't have a mink coat. But she does have a respectable Republican cloth coat, and I always tell her that she would look good in anything."

Then he told the public about Checkers, a little cocker spaniel, "black and white, spotted," sent by a man down in Texas who had heard Pat say the children would like to have a dog. "And you know, the kids, like all kids, loved the dog, and I just want to say this, right now, that regardless of what they say about it, we are going to keep it."

Nixon was going to "continue this fight. I am going to campaign up and down America until we drive the crooks and the Communists and those that defend them out of Washington." Nodding to Pat, he said she was "not a quitter. After all, her name was Patricia Ryan and she was born on Saint Patrick's Day, and you know the Irish never quit." Nor did most Americans share what seemed to be the view of Democratic National Chairman Stephen Mitchell who "says that only a rich man should serve in the Government." It was fine for someone like Governor Stevenson, with his inherited fortune, but remember what Abe Lincoln said, "God must have loved the common people, he made so many of them."

A contemptuous minority derided the speech as the unctuous performance of a Uriah Heep. What followed constituted a unique experience for the Republican National Committee. That the broadcast went off the air before Nixon could give the mailing address of the national committee only strengthened its impact. Not knowing where to turn, listeners reached out to whatever seemed plausible. Calls and telegrams inundated Republican offices everywhere; in desperation, respondents also turned to local television and radio stations.

Within the next few days, the national committee received more than 200,000 letters, a load that kept nearly 100 volunteers working for a month, even overflowing across half the lobby of the Washington Hotel. Out of those envelopes came some $62,000 in contributions. More than 160,000 telegrams were delivered to the main headquarters of the Republican National Committee alone. For every anti-Nixon response, there were 350 in his favor. The Luce publications, which had been sympathetic throughout the crisis, followed through with a seven-page spread in *Life* that was headlined, "Nixon Fights, Wins and Weeps."

Ike then sent Nixon a telegram in which praise for the "magnificent" performance was coupled with words signifying that the ultimate decision would be his rather than the numbers reported by the national committee. He also asked Nixon to join him at Wheeling, West Virginia, his next campaign stop. Because of the flood of telegrams, Nixon did not receive Eisenhower's and was unaware of even its qualified commendation. His only word came from a news report that stressed the general's continued determination to delay making a decision, which infuriated him. Nixon would not go crawling to the general, he warned, to beg forgiveness and meekly await his judgment. He was, in fact, ready to resign; meanwhile, he would resume his own campaign schedule, moving on to Missoula, and ignore Eisenhower's request to meet him in Wheeling. That was it; there was no further time for discussion; it was time to go to the airport.

The brouhaha was, in effect, all over. Republican National Committee Chairman Arthur Summerfield found after talking to Eisenhower in Portsmouth, Ohio, that the general wanted to know where the national committee stood. Taking a quick telephone poll from Wheeling, he found that all 107 who were reached favored keeping Nixon. The information was immediately wired to Eisenhower on his campaign train, and the decision was made. Summerfield and Humphreys got on the phone to Nixon with assurances that Eisenhower was ready to greet him with his full support. Summerfield then relayed the good news to Sherman Adams at the "next Ike Special stop," Ironton, Ohio.

When Richard and Pat Nixon reached West Virginia, they were astonished to find Eisenhower running up to them ready to shake hands. "What are you doing here, General? You didn't have to come out to the airport to meet us," said Nixon. "Why not?" said Ike with a big grin and an arm around his running mate. "You're my boy!"

Vice President

On election day, Nixon walked alone with Bill Rogers along the scenic ridge overlooking the ocean at Laguna Beach. Then the returns confirmed the Eisenhower-Nixon victory. Not since Herbert Hoover's defeat of Al Smith in 1928 had Republicans swept their way to national power. Their ticket's 55 percent of the popular vote, combined with a 221 to 213 control of the new House, effectively dispatched Stevenson and his Democrats. As the incoming vice president, moreover, Nixon would be in the position of casting the decisive vote in the Senate and give his party the winning margin in case of a tie.

As Nixon wrote in his pre-presidential "retirement" memoir, *Six Crises*, what really happened was far more significant, for both himself and his party. The administration had taken pride in teamwork, thereby minimizing impressions of Eisenhower's importance in decision making. But at the same time, the American people still needed to know that he *was* the president, which left Nixon as little more than a symbolic surrogate.

Six Crises hinted at other complications. "There is an old political axiom," Nixon wrote, "that where a vacuum exists, it will be filled by the nearest or strongest power. That had to be avoided at all costs." There could be no "semblance of a struggle for dominance." Scrambles for power, he acknowledged, had taken place in earlier administrations and, despite the "staff system" that ran Eisenhower's "team," such conflicts appeared "to be taking hold in the present one." Precedent appeared to predestine Nixon to the innocuous role that FDR's first vice president, John Nance Garner, had once described as "not worth a bowl of warm spit." Eisenhower, the military commander, had, moreover, installed his own barrier around the Oval Office by creating a gatekeeper with the title of chief of staff, occupied by the crusty and austere former New Hampshire governor, Sherman Adams. He also had a powerful, avuncular secretary of state, John Foster Dulles. The heir to a family of diplomats, Dulles's personal authority profited from the impression that he was the administration's strongman, a plus for Eisenhower's still uncertain credibility as a bona fide Republican.

Nixon fell into that atmosphere by playing his role and playing it well, becoming the most active and the most influential vice president the nation had yet seen. His indisputable achievement was to rescue the image of his office away from the sort of burlesque that the nation had digested in the Pulitzer Prize–winning 1931 satirical musical of the White House by George and Ira Gershwin, *Of Thee I Sing*. Comic actor Victor Moore long remained in the minds of many as the caricature of a feeble, incompetent vice president with no other talent than awaiting the death of the man in the Oval Office.

Circumstances and the Eisenhower style quickly contributed to the making of Vice President Nixon as a credible team player. By statute, thanks to the National Security Act of 1947, Nixon's position made him a member of the new National Security Council, which immediately elevated the traditional role his office could play. Moreover, there was the prominence of the Far East in

Cold War diplomacy, especially with the empowerment of the People's Republic of China and the continuing war in Korea. Most observers thought that Eisenhower effectively clinched the election by dramatically promising to "go to Korea" if he won. Making good on that promise, he visited the war front in December.

On July 27, 1953, six months after Eisenhower's inauguration, fighting stopped on the Korean peninsula, not by a formal armistice but by a simple cease-fire along the line of battle that roughly corresponded to the thirty-eighth parallel, which had been the political division of Korea in the first place. The arrangement was, in effect, a stalemate, deferring complex issues until some later, unspecified date. But it did end the killing, killing that had cost some 37,000 American lives. Sufficient to fulfill an implicit campaign pledge without producing a "victory" that the administration could celebrate in public, it nevertheless opened the way to great diplomatic maneuverability along the Pacific Rim, especially with the Communist regime in Beijing.

It was also no trivial matter for the president to dispatch his second in command to Asia only a few months after the cease-fire. Nixon traveled with Pat and went off on a ten-week tour of 19 countries, giving him a central role in the focal point that had become Southeast Asia.

The success of his mission confirmed the stature of the young vice president. Right after Christmas of 1953, shortly after returning to the States, he delivered a nationwide TV and radio report to the American people that laid out the accomplishments, dangers, and ideals. Taking a partisan swipe at his Democratic predecessors, he argued that "If China had not gone Communist, we would not have had a war in Korea." Alluding to the administration's continuing crisis in the region, he added that "there would now be no war in Indochina, and there would be no war in

Malaya." Nixon's performance served as an early lift for his foreign policy credentials.

On April 16, 1954, at a forum held by the American Society of Newspaper Editors, his remarks about Southeast Asia and Dien Bien Phu under the French situation "stirred anxieties within both the administration and the Congress, distressed the American people and . . . created new questions about exactly what Eisenhower and Dulles were planning to do about France's deteriorating colonial position." A large French force had been under siege at Dien Bien Phu since November.

Nixon called the possible use of American troops an assumption and said he doubted it would happen. Then, instead of evading a hypothetical question, he replied that "the United States is the leader of the free world, and the free world cannot afford in Asia a further retreat to the Communists. . . . if in order to avoid it, we must take the risk now by putting American boys in, I believe that the executive branch of the government has to take the politically unpopular position of facing up to it and doing it, and I personally would support such a decision."

Although they were supposedly given "off the record," his remarks, when revealed in the next day's papers, were shocking. Fighting in Korea had stopped only months earlier, and the public was ignorant about Operation Vulture, aware of American financial aid going to the French, but unaware of any possible U. S. military intervention. Nixon's suggestion suddenly opened a new and frightening possibility. Support was hard to find. Eisenhower's press secretary, Jim Hagerty, who privately called the statement "foolish," immediately said he could not confirm that Nixon had reflected the president's view. He simply had no knowledge of the story. In Georgia, where Eisenhower was in the temporary White House on the grounds of the Augusta National Golf Club, Dulles hurriedly conferred with the president about how to handle the protests without weakening his bargaining position with the Communist diplomats at Geneva. His solution was to tell reporters that the use of U.S. troops was "unlikely" but not impossible. Defense Secretary Charles Wilson added that his department did not intend to send troops to Indochina. Key legislative leaders of both parties all joined in denying that the United States was about to have "another Korea." The publication of Gallup's first post-comment survey merely confirmed what the reactions had already made obvious. Thirty years later, Nixon explained that he was just speculating about actions that were already on the table and in tune with "the Eisenhower-Dulles management of foreign policy, contributing to the cultivation of deliberate ambiguity, a tactic that worked particularly well in the Far East."

Nixon and Dulles worried more about Republican conservatives than about the Democrats. The two men also drew close; Nixon later recalled Dulles as the best friend he had in the Eisenhower cabinet. Clearly, he was undergoing extensive tutelage in foreign policy. He not only regarded the older man, the diplomatic specialist "born to be secretary of state," as his strongest supporter in the cabinet, but pointed out that their relationship only deepened when a heart attack temporarily sidelined the president. Or, as has been pointed out in a more critical sense, "Nixon became Dulles's match in foreign policy, "pushing his views, and even infringing on Dulles's territory, always, however, remaining a loyal member of the team. In a sense, the vice president became a third wheel in the formulation of how the administration presented itself to the rest of the world."

The heart attack that struck Eisenhower in September 1955 was another one of Nixon's "six crises." Those weeks in the fall of 1955 were anxious ones. Reports from Fitzsimons Army Hospital in Colorado kept updating the president's progress and held the key to the vice president's own political future. But the lack of any constitutional definitions about presidential incapacity made the situation vastly more complex. In circumstances with deep political implications, Nixon had to avoid even the appearance of seeming to be overeager.

Given the delicacy of his situation, he had to have the savvy to understand the difference between discretion and weakness. In mid-October, with many of the immediate difficulties having been resolved, he wrote to a colleague that his "primary concern has been to avoid allowing any doubt to be raised." Fortunately, for the nation and the Republican party, good news kept coming from the hospital. The president had intended to serve only one term; now, he might not only be able to complete his four years but also allow himself to be re-nominated in 1956. As the public was constantly reassured, the "team" had carried on in his absence, the nation had not suffered, and all would soon return to normal.

"You are the constitutional second-in-command and you ought to assume the leadership," Nixon was reminded by Senator Styles Bridges. Bridges, a New Hampshire rival of Sherman Adams, was eager to check the power of the chief of staff. He urged against letting "the White House clique take command." Bridges was not alone. He and other Nixon supporters had certainly seen the dispatch sent to the *New York Times* only one day after Eisenhower's heart attack that suggested that the president's men would be doing everything possible to make sure that interim power went not to the constitutional second in command but to Adams.

Behind Adams was John Foster Dulles. That was the moment when Dulles's political maneuvering was far more significant than anything he had ever done about foreign policy. He was, as Nixon later told an interviewer, the general above everybody else. No moves were made during that period without checking in with Dulles.

In the face of the dilemma created by the presidential illness, Dulles was not about to permit a possible vacancy in the executive office to be filled by a vice president whose selection had been prompted by the need to appeal to the Republican right. Dulles, clearly backed by Eisenhower, was also firm about keeping Nixon as a figurehead.

Nixon acted accordingly. Right after press secretary Jim Hagerty reached him that Saturday night with the news about the heart attack, he avoided the press. He spent that first night secluded in the Bethesda home of old friend Bill Rogers, then Eisenhower's acting attorney general. For the sake of appearances, not least of which was the orchestration of the business-as-usual posture, Nixon presided over both the National Security Council and the cabinet. Meanwhile, Dulles used the emergency to enhance the policy-making functions of the NSC.

By the time the crisis ended, the vice president had the first inkling that he was the one whose ambitions were going to have to be placed under tighter control. The sacrificial lamb was being readied for slaughter. Where the administration had succeeded in its first three years— ending the Korean War, pulling the economy out of a brief recession, establishing an opening with the Soviets via "the spirit of Geneva" not very long after Stalin's death—Nixon's name was absent from the credits.

The negatives fell disproportionately on his side of the table. Even before the administration's start, there had been a considerable pileup. Eisenhower's "high road" approach was balanced by the vice president's mission to arouse the party's more passionate supporters, especially on the political right. When Joe McCarthy had to be told off before the American people, the assignment went to Nixon, and it was he who did the work of going public with the first open estrangement between the administration and the buccaneering senator. When, only a few days later, a plan for rescuing the French from impending disaster in Southeast Asia circulated within the administration's high command, it fell to Nixon to float a controversial trial balloon suggesting that American ground forces might be needed in Indochina. More than anybody else in the administration, it was Nixon who campaigned for congressional Republicans in 1954 by carrying out his function as the man who could rally fervent anti-Communists. When the Republicans lost their brief Senate majority as a result of that midterm election, the onus was also Nixon's. The party's right wing, already dismayed by the formal condemnation of Joe McCarthy in late 1954, lost further confidence in the administration when Eisenhower parlayed with Georgi Malenkov and Nikita Khrushchev at the Geneva summit meeting in July 1955.

One thing had become clear by the time Eisenhower had his heart attack: The effort to reinforce the appeal to Republican conservatives confirmed the Nixon stereotype as a hard-line, right-wing street fighter. Simultaneously, moves toward healing Cold War tensions provoked distrust among those who feared betrayal of the party's anti-Communist principles. Recalling that many conservatives had supported him only because of the Hiss case, Nixon later said, "What concerns me about the far right is their tendency to see everything in terms of black and white." Paradoxically, so cantankerous a commentator on the left as journalist I. F. Stone, noting how far to the right some elements were bulging, wrote that Nixon had "become a middle-of-the-road spokesman and conservative papers like the *Washington Star* and *New York Times* find themselves classified more and more as part of the 'left-wing press.'"

Nixon played his role well. Delicate situation and all, made even touchier by his reputation for opportunism, one can nevertheless hardly find anything questionable about his conduct during those weeks of Eisenhower's recuperation. The administration and the country needed a good soldier, and he was the man. He agreed with Dulles that the recent renunciation of force by the Communist regime in Peking should be acknowledged. He was also relieved to step out of his role as a hatchet man.

When Nixon delivered the closing speech of the annual *Herald Tribune* forum in New York on world affairs, his language was moderate, carefully balanced, without strident partisanship, and lacking in bellicose fervor; he didn't even fault the Democrats for "losing" China. The speech, described by the *Times* as "more Eisenhower than Nixon" and as the product of advice from friends urging that he become more unifying than divisive, was not even suspected as having been influenced by Dulles.

Clearly, Nixon was being whipsawed between the inevitability of his succession if Eisenhower should be unable to complete his term—or, at the very least, the possibility of retaining his spot on the ticket in 1956—and the considerable pressures that were being applied to get him to step aside and take a cabinet post, a suggestion that came directly from the president. He was too controversial, had too many enemies and was a liability to the ticket in the eyes of some influential Republicans. And Eisenhower, being Eisenhower, was not about to be pressured into any decisions before they were absolutely necessary. Nixon's dilemma would have been hard for any man. For someone with his pride and sensitivity, the experience was especially galling. Not until Minnesota's former governor, Harold Stassen, who had done everything to stop Nixon's renomination, even going so far as to suggest that he could be replaced by Massachusetts Governor Christian Herter (and with what also looked like Eisenhower's approval), finally called for unity at the San Francisco convention, was he assured of a second term. The Eisenhower-Nixon team, running on a "peace and prosperity" theme, comfortably defeated another Democratic challenge from Adlai Stevenson and his running mate, Senator Estes Kefauver of Tennessee.

Re-election in 1956 came amid two unrelated crises, both significant, unexpected, and from abroad. Soviet troops, after a forced brief withdrawal, brutally suppressed an uprising by Hungarian "freedom fighters." Despite frantic pleas by the rebels for American assistance in trying to maintain their temporary liberation, the Eisenhower administration was embarrassingly unresponsive. All that jingoistic partisan talk of deliverance for the "captive peoples" was suddenly forgotten. Nixon, with misgivings about that past, recalled his own role.

"I was the one who developed the phrase about Khrushchev being the 'butcher of Budapest,'" he said many years later. "I had been saying that over and over again. Then, here we come in with Suez. What do I say about the British and the French? So coming after that, I thought 'what terrible timing.' Attention suddenly shifted to the Suez Canal."

Just as Eisenhower and Nixon faced their re-election, the administration confronted a war it did not want and could not control. Israelis, harassed by murderous attacks launched by *fedayeen* (guerrilla) raiders from across the Gaza Strip, suddenly lashed back, rushing troops toward the Sinai Peninsula and the Suez Canal. Egypt's dictator, Gamal Abdul Nasser, placing himself at the head of pan-Arab nationalism and rallying the Middle East against the Jewish state and European interests, had been spurned by both Great Britain and the United States when he tried to win the financing necessary to build a high dam at Aswan.

Given the American interest in "evenhandedness" in the Middle East, and given their anxieties about both Soviet influence and access to the region's oil, that was not the time to help Nasser finance his dam. Firmly, in July, Dulles threw the deal back in the face of the ambassador from Cairo when he came for the money.

With no funding for Aswan from Washington and the British troops gone, only one week after Dulles's rejection Nasser nationalized control of Suez, immediately canceling the principle of the canal as an international waterway and raising the specter of its closure at his pleasure.

Nasser's move, aimed at least in part at using canal tolls to help finance a high dam at Aswan, astonished Eisenhower along with everybody else in Washington. It also confirmed the failure of the administration's policy, not only with the Egyptians but also with the British, who had once had thousands of troops helping protect the waterway. But the immediate effect was the determination of both London and Paris to react with force. Would American policy be once again held hostage to the Israeli vote? That was Dulles's dilemma. Not if he could help it. Nor did they have much confidence that the votes of American Jews would be theirs in any event. Nixon, who was consulted on every step by Dulles as events in the Middle East unfolded, agreed that politics might create an anti-Arab policy once again. However much it might alienate certain groups, he held, the matter should be dealt with on a nonpartisan basis. David Ben-Gurion's government in Tel Aviv, after some hesitation about going ahead with the war before the American election, evidently hoped such political considerations would inhibit official interference before Israel and its Western allies could accomplish their mission, failing to take seriously Eisenhower's warning that "we would handle our affairs as though we didn't have a Jew in America."

But the Israelis, having lost the support of the Russians which they had had at their nation's birth, also needed to live with the reality that it was often only by chance that their needs coincided with the interests of their Western friends. The Suez Canal, neutralized and open to international shipping since 1888, was one specific case. That waterway, the vital passage through to the Mediterranean from Middle East oil fields, had since 1948 been denied to their maritime traffic by the Egyptian government. Among European powers with material interests in the area were the British and French, who feared that they, too, might lose such rights. Along with most of the West, they particularly dreaded the loss of Arab oil, and so did the Americans. As Eisenhower noted in his diary, "The oil of the Arab world has grown increasingly important to all of Europe. The economy of European countries would collapse if those oil supplies were cut off," and, if that happened, "the United States would be in a situation of which the difficulty could scarcely be exaggerated."

On the October 31, Nixon called Dulles from Detroit to say that it was more important to reassert firmness and dispel any notion that America had a "pipsqueak" as president than to worry about how Jews would react. The Republicans didn't have enough of that vote to make a difference anyway. Small countries had to be kept independent while preventing American troops from becoming involved. That was the point to make, he urged the secretary: Reports that tied military action in the area to the failure of our policy must be countered by our assertion of non-interventionism.

On November 5, with the Israeli conquest of the Sinai Peninsula and the Gaza Strip complete except for minor mopping-up operations, an Anglo-French airdrop began at Port Said, followed by amphibious landings the next day. Four armies fought on Egyptian soil, all in defiance of Washington's wishes, or even knowledge. The tri-nation attacks were, moreover, obviously coordinated.

The Russians, even while crushing the Hungarian rebellion in Budapest, also pressed demands for withdrawal, pointing out that London and Paris were within range of their nuclear weapons. Even more ominous, and sternly rebuffed by Eisenhower, was Khrushchev's proposal for a joint U.S.–Soviet military operation to crush the "aggression against Egypt." By the next day, Moscow was announcing that their "volunteers" were applying to serve with Nasser's soldiers. On November 7, the day after American voters reelected the Eisenhower-Nixon ticket, the three invaders accepted the cease-fire calls. Their forces halted short of the canal, with the waterway itself still in Egyptian hands but clogged and disabled by the wreckage of ships. American opposition, UN resolutions, and, finally, the threats of Russian intervention, were too much. Nixon, prevented by the political campaign from having much of a say in what was going on, was most visible as a spokesman, a role he served in direct connection with Dulles.

The secretary wired ahead to Nixon at Hershey, Pennsylvania, where he was due to deliver a televised campaign speech before 3,000 people at the local arena. Adlai Stevenson had just called the administration's Middle East policy a failure and charged that the president should have been able to avert the crisis. As a result, claimed the Democratic presidential candidate, the United States stood alone "in an unfriendly world." Dulles forwarded harder-hitting language to counter such criticism, words that were bound to make headlines. Just before election day, the secretary obviously felt the need to defend the administration's Middle East position in the strongest possible way. Not since the start of the Cold War had the United States parted so openly from its principal Western allies and even found itself on the same side as the Soviet Union. Nixon, loyally attempting to turn a diplomatic setback to the administration's advantage, used Dulles's words and explained that "for the first time in history we have shown independence of Anglo-French policies which seemed to us to reflect the colonial tradition. That declaration of independence has had an electrifying effect throughout the world." It was, in short, as Nixon reminded his audience, a sign of our strength. "The moment we are weak we invite war."

In Washington, Dulles, back from a long round of debates at the United Nations in New York, had severe stomach pains late that night. Rushed to Walter Reed Hospital the next morning, he was in surgery for two and a half hours. Instead of finding what they hoped were kidney stones, doctors cut away a malignant growth that was piercing his abdomen.

Nixon's private views were often complex; for anyone close to him, it was natural to suspect that, at heart, he had considerable admiration for the Israeli and Anglo-French initiative. Even given the importance of unifying behind the team, he was then simply too far from the scene where policy was being decided, and he had little choice, especially when campaigning, except to support the White House and the State Department. Moreover, he simply went along with the decision.

Two decades later, a more experienced Nixon came to believe that "our actions were a serious mistake. Nasser became even more rash and aggressive than before, and the seeds of another Mideast war were planted." Eisenhower, too, he later reported, came to believe he had made a mistake. When his British counterpart paid him a hospital visit, Dulles regretted that he had not given the nod to America's allies to go ahead and take the canal instead of conceding it to the Egyptians.

There was inadequate awareness of Nixon's emergence as a distinct force. The irony was that, while still very far from those on the extreme right who actually saw Dulles and Eisenhower as betrayers of U.S. interests, Nixon also doubted that their responses were firm enough to meet long-term demands. He could and did welcome the end of fighting in Korea and the avoidance of American bloodshed at Dien Bien Phu, just as he was also relieved that East and West stopped short of a violent showdown over Suez. Each case, however, left him with the uncomfortable feeling that, as FDR had found convenient to do when dealing with the Russians at Yalta, areas of serious conflict were merely being postponed. His anxieties would doubtlessly have been greater had he been prescient enough to know how many of those issues would one day land on his desk in the Oval Office.

One major consequence of the U.S.-UN-Soviet reaction to Suez was the forced withdrawal of Israeli armies to the original boundaries that had been established by the United Nations in 1948. With the immediate crisis over, the administration initiated a Middle Eastern replica of the Formosa Resolution, this one bearing the name of the president. The original resolution authorized the president "to employ the armed forces of the United States as he deems necessary" to defend Formosa (Taiwan) and the offshore islands. Precisely what would trigger a military response by the U.S. was left undefined, a ploy designed to "keep them guessing."

Nixon, for his part, increased his own efforts to play a more conspicuous role. The time had come to do more than, as he put it, serve as Dulles's "political eyes and ears." If he could be something like an executive assistant, that would be fine. But that, of course, risked stepping on the toes of other powers. What might be best, Eisenhower ventured, would be helping to prepare legislation dealing with national security matters. Nixon agreed, pointing to his congressional experience, foreign travels, and service as a member of the National Security Council as qualifications. In any event, the president wanted any enhancement to take place without formal publicity.

The real change had little to do with constitutional functions of the vice presidency or impingement of powers over any particular department or agency. Nixon took his "political eyes and ears" overseas. Travel, all coordinated with Secretary Dulles, became a more prominent function of his office than for any previous vice president, reflecting, no doubt, how both the world and his office had changed. There was also Nixon's insatiable curiosity and zest for involvement. He was, for example, present at the unveiling of the new African state of Ghana.

Much better publicized, and of infinitely greater political value, was his 1958 trip to Latin America. A key figure in an administration that supported rightist Latin dictatorships, Nixon became a natural target for anger at Yankee imperialism. Protests, no doubt fanned by local Communist activists but fed as much by history, placed Nixon and his wife under siege and, at times, perilously close to physical harm. The violence was especially fierce in Caracas, where enraged students rocked their automobile and threatened to maul the occupants. The Nixons were also spat upon—undignified, insulting, but not life-threatening; still, a nightmare for all concerned, not least for those who were assigned to protect the visitors.

In his ceremonial duties, Nixon had become the man on the firing line. He was also, at the same time, an adjunct to the secretary of state, doing those things that Dulles thought he should not do for himself. Cancer forced Dulles to give up his State Department post in April 1959, and he died in May at the age of seventy-one. Nixon, by then, already absorbed by his future political prospects, was far more of a foreign policy buff than he had ever been in California.

Defeat

Vice President Nixon was still Ike's boy; in 1958, he was at the center of the administration's second-term crisis. Eisenhower remained the national hero, but illness—especially a serious intestinal blockage and a stroke, all after his heart attack in 1955—continued to plague the thirty-fourth president. His comforting charm had become somewhat worn, even drab, as he turned older and grayer.

There was, it seemed, an end to his famous "luck." The Russians, with no advance fanfare, successfully launched an outer space satellite named *Sputnik*, earning them respect for the sort of technical "expertise" traditionally associated with the West. Scandal forced the resignation of his indispensable chief of staff, Sherman Adams. Far more damaging, however, was the wobbly economy. A combination of inflation and recession—stagflation, it came to be called—took a further toll on his popularity. That year, 1958, also brought renewed anxiety over the islands of Quemoy and Matsu, just off the Chinese coast and still claimed by Chiang Kai-shek and his Nationalists. As long as that continued, American intervention remained an open possibility. Marines were also dispatched to Lebanon to counter any possible Soviet military meddling. The city of Berlin, divided since the war into eastern and western sectors, remained the most potential flash point for a potential World War III.

At the same time, surveys generally showed that voters were either preoccupied with pocketbook issues or just tuned out. When a Gallup poll asked how much attention they were giving to the elections, 59 percent said "little" or "none." The slumping economy was of more immediate concern. Nixon despaired that winning the 1960 nomination might very well turn out to be worthless.

After the 1958 congressional elections, serious setbacks for Republicans, the vice president increased his involvement in foreign policy. As Eisenhower and Khrushchev contemplated their conciliatory exchange visits, Nixon went to Russia at the president's request, met the Communist leader and, most famously, engaged him in the so-called "kitchen debate" at Moscow's Sokolniki Park. They debated the relative merits of the U.S. and Russian ways of life.

The encounter was a bonanza for the vice president. Images of Nixon lecturing Khrushchev about American economic superiority traveled around the globe. Viewers could see for themselves how he "stood up" to the Soviet leader, appearing to confront him as an equal. Nixon had won his most important round yet.

His gambit paid off. Inevitably, Republicans turned to him, leaving the Californian with the job of contesting a relative newcomer to national politics, Senator John F. Kennedy of Massachusetts. Kennedy had won his seat only eight years earlier, and had not established a very remarkable record. But in his skillful fight to get to the top, he managed to beat out the two-time Democratic loser, Adlai Stevenson, as well as Senate Majority Leader Lyndon Johnson.

Nixon had to remain loyal to the record of the past eight years. He differed only cautiously, as when he sided with the Democrats about the need for stronger defenses. Such gestures of independence were easily overshadowed by his ties to the president. Eisenhower's delayed entry as an active campaigner for him raised more doubts about the older man's enthusiasm for Nixon, who worried about being caught in a squeeze between Rockefeller moderates and Goldwater conservatives. Mere recognition of a need to define national goals placed Nixon in the position of implying that America had somehow lost its way under Ike. Kennedy managed to out-maneuver his Republican opponents by putting them on the defensive about the adequacy of national security.

A high point of the campaign, then a novelty, featured a series of four debates carried by both television and radio. The vice president, in contrast to Kennedy, was poorly served by his make-up people. Seeming to need a shave (having a "five o'clock shadow" was a popular term at the time) and with a visage that projected something sinister to those who preferred to see him that way, he clearly lost out to the younger man, whose crisp command of his material projected strength in contrast to Nixon's vagueness and efforts to be agreeable.

That first televised presidential debate attracted more than 100 million viewers. Many of those who only heard it over radio, not television, were more impressed by Nixon's verbal performance. But, as well as many thought he did in the subsequent debates, he never really recovered.

Nixon remained on the defensive. Kennedy hammered away on "the need to get America moving again" and the importance of regaining America's "fallen" prestige. He even charged, later acknowledged to be deceptive, that the United States had fallen behind the Soviet Union because a "missile gap" was weakening America. A Kennedy administration, he made clear, would not continue to tolerate the existence of a Fidel Castro in Cuba.

Kennedy's own bellicosity was made more plausible by the apparent weakening of the Eisenhower–Nixon administration. The Soviet launching of their outer space missile seemed to elevate their military capabilities, just as their smashing of the Hungarian revolt in 1956 had reasserted the dominance of the Soviet bloc over Eastern Europe. Eisenhower's acknowledgment of responsibility of the U-2 incident, in which the spy plane navigated by Francis Gary Powers was embarrassingly brought to the ground in the heart of the Soviet Union, was a humiliating pre-election diplomatic setback.

The outcome was among the most indecisive in American history. Nixon later emphasized the narrow margin: scarcely more than 100,000 popular votes out of more than 68 million, a difference of just 2 percent. Fraudulent counting in a number of places, especially in Texas and Illinois, where Chicago mayor Richard Daley had reportedly reassured Kennedy that "with a little bit of luck and the help of a few close friends, you're going to carry Illinois," could easily have deprived Nixon of an actual popular plurality. Even a more judicious distribution of the two-candidate vote that went to unpledged electors in some southern states can be used to demonstrate that more voters actually cast their ballots for a Nixon victory. One method developed by *Congressional Quarterly* gave Nixon a national popular vote margin of 58,181—little wonder why he believed that he was *not* rejected by the American people.

The most responsible factor, Nixon later argued, was the downturn of the economy. Eisenhower, he pointed out in an interview, went below 50 percent approval for the first time in 1958, "and that was because of the recession," which hurt GOP candidates badly in that year's mid-term elections. A Gallup poll released just before Americans were set to vote for the presidency in 1960 that asked whether individuals thought they would be better off financially with a Democratic or with a Republican victory reported that 51 percent of the respondents chose the Democrats and just 35 percent the Republicans.

Where conditions were depressed, especially in urban regions of the Northeast, Kennedy's vote was one sided. As the count piled up, it became obvious that pocketbook worries were more likely than religion to drive voters toward Kennedy. In city after city, Nixon's vote correlated more with high unemployment than with anti-Catholicism.

The debate over Illinois, however, lived on. Nixon, in his post-election account, enumerates the precincts where votes outnumbered voters. Mayor Daley surely managed to withhold returns until he knew just how many votes would be needed for a statewide plurality. The overall Kennedy advantage in Chicago was a healthy 450,000; statewide, fewer than 9,000. His Texas edge was much more substantial, 46,233. Altogether, a total of 51 electoral votes were at stake in the two states, 24 in Texas alone. Nixon added up the pluses and minuses of challenging the outcome, and decided to let the vote stand. Not only Illinois, but also Texas would have had to be reversed for Nixon to get an Electoral College majority.

* * *

Beginning to dominate Republican politics was the appeal of the Goldwater drive. For Goldwater, there were few compromises. He outdid Nixon as a cold warrior, identifying himself ever more closely with militarism and bellicosity. He called for the GOP to move to the right because they had gone about as far to the left as they could go. He championed the South, states' rights, and opposition to federal intervention in race relations, allowing, in other words, racist segregation patterns to go unchallenged. In Goldwater, labor leaders had their most tenacious opponent. He had stood fast with the 21 other Republicans who resisted the Senate's condemnation of Senator Joe McCarthy. A wealthy member of a merchant family, Goldwater also had rugged good looks and spoke as plainly about his convictions as any politician since Harry Truman, while avoiding the excesses common to many on the far right. He kept his head, recognized that Nixon would be better than any Democrat, and puffed new hope into the hearts of those who, like John Bricker of Ohio, thought that "the American people are ready for a revival of some real old fashioned patriotism."

Nixon's loss, difficult as it was for him to accept, left him fair game for Goldwater or New York Governor Nelson Rockefeller, a man so rich and so powerful that one can understand how hard it would be for him to comprehend that the world was not his. Contemporary estimates of Rockefeller suggested $100 million to $200 million as his personal worth, all part of some $2 billion to $3 billion in family assets. He took over the government at Albany and immediately converted the state and the inherited Republican Party into a Rockefeller manor. For all that, it was becoming obviously clear, perhaps to everybody but him, that all the money in the world would not enable him to break into Goldwater's waltz with grassroots Republicans. Large numbers of social conservatives were, moreover, offended when the governor quickly took another wife soon after divorcing his first.

Nixon, meanwhile, not swearing off politics altogether, much to Pat's distress, returned to Whittier and his California base. He became a senior partner in a law firm with a guaranteed income that totaled more than his 14-year earnings in Washington, or about $350,000, and, appropriately enough for an ex-vice president of the United States, settled in with his family in an upscale section of Los Angeles overlooking Beverly Hills. He paid for his new ranch-style, four-bedroom house in part from the sale of his old place and partly, to his future embarrassment, from a loan by Teamsters labor boss, Jimmy Hoffa.

Off to a comfortable start back in California, and at the age of forty-eight, he and Pat could have settled in for a comfortable life, practicing law, raising their daughters, Julie and Tricia, and enjoying celebrity status on the West Coast. One can easily imagine Pat's anxiety. He had, after all, promised early retirement from political life. Now he weighed getting into it all again—and after running for the presidency—this time to unseat the incumbent governor of California, Pat Brown; not, in any way, a simple decision.

He was well aware, as he told a friend, that he might be "committing political hari kari as far as running for any future political office is concerned." He would rather keep his options open, but he had no real choice. By not running, he would, in effect, remove himself from a serious political role, a point repeated by fellow Republicans, from Ike on down.

He entered the governorship race, fully aware of the dangers, including his lack of preparation for dealing with statewide issues. He also suffered from the widespread suspicion that he was using the governorship race as a stepping-stone to the presidency. He was also stung, as he later claimed, when he turned off elements of California's far right by distancing himself from some of the state's more paranoid anti-Communist followers of the increasingly popular John Birch Society. There was no real issue that he could use against Brown, and he was further undermined when the Cuban missile crisis, with its potential for nuclear war with the Soviet Union, riveted attention. Brown, demonstrating the importance of his incumbency in fulfilling his responsibilities, flew to Washington to be at the president's "side." Going into election day, Nixon figured that Brown was drawing just enough to win. Brown actually emerged somewhat stronger than that. Nixon's total fell some 297,000 short out of six million votes cast.

Most of the pain came not from the loss itself but from a self-inflicted wound suffered the morning after Californians voted. After withholding a concession statement and "exhausted mentally and physically" from the night before and appearing "hung over, trembling and red-eyed," as well as "emotionally fatigued," Nixon reluctantly went down to meet the waiting press at his Beverly Hilton headquarters. His remarks rambled, betraying—some thought—the several glasses of scotch he had had the night before.

He concluded by telling the assembled journalists that they would not have "Nixon to kick around anymore, because, gentlemen, this is my last press conference and it will be one in which I have welcomed the opportunity to test wits with you." Even worse, only a few days earlier, he had kind words for the press's coverage of the campaign, and with good reason. "He clearly had given up," remembered a long-time aide, and hardly anybody thought he had a political future. How many crises could he endure?

Coincidentally, his first book, *Six Crises*, a memoir that traced his experiences from the Hiss case through his loss to Kennedy, also came out that year. Throughout its discussion of each case, Nixon made clear that the ability to respond to crises was the real test of leadership, a theme that he hit hard in his later works. Recalling the Checkers speech, the California loss, in all reality, despite his "sacrifice" as a good party man, stood unwritten as Nixon's "eighth crisis."

* * *

"Nobody wanted to stay," Julie Nixon later recalled. At least for that moment, Nixon seemed to have given up on politics.

So they went to New York, the land of Rockefeller Republicanism. Even in that world, with a high-power legal circle comparable only to the national capital itself, Richard Nixon was a heavy hitter. "A lot of lawyers," one friend was quoted as having said at the time, "didn't want a tiger in their midst."

He arrived with the best kind of credentials, the sort of connections guaranteed to boost the revenue of even such a high-power law firm as Mudge, Stern, Baldwin, and Todd. With offices at 20 Broad Street, in the heart of New York City's financial district, its business included such major clients as Warner-Lambert, the pharmaceutical house. It did not hurt that its board chairman was a Nixon vice presidential friend, Elmer Bobst, as was another friend, Donald Kendall, the head of Pepsi-Cola. Kendall confirmed that it was he and Bobst who helped get Nixon the senior partnership "by giving them my business." The firm's revised letterheads read "Nixon, Mudge, Rose, Guthrie, and Alexander." He also made two long-term connections at Mudge, Rose; one was John Mitchell, who later joined his presidential cabinet as attorney general; the other was Leonard Garment, who became a friend and adviser, and a liberal presence in the Nixon circle.

Political activism in his new state was, of course, out of the question, especially since three key local Republicans, Rockefeller, Senator Jacob Javits, and Mayor John Lindsay, "totally froze him out of all state events," as Julie Nixon has put it. He applied himself diligently to the business of law, to finally earning big money by handling high-powered cases, and giving talks. One of them, at London's Guild Hall, championed American foreign policy to an audience of European skeptics and, as one Nixon friend recalled, "left them eating out of his hands."

Affluent for the first time in his life, Nixon moved Pat and the girls into a ten-room cooperative apartment on Fifth Avenue, coincidentally as a neighbor of Nelson Rockefeller. "Rocky" was beginning to symbolize what was happening to the GOP. To a new generation of conservatives, then largely lining up behind Goldwater, the term "Rockefeller Republicans" was becoming an epithet, the epitome of "moderation" or even "liberalism."

Nobody could have anticipated the sometimes bizarre sequence of events that followed. On November 23, 1963, Nixon had just returned from a Pepsi-Cola board meeting in Dallas. He was still in the cab en route from the airport to Manhattan when he got the news that President John F. Kennedy had just been shot in that Texas city. When he left the car in front of his building, the doorman confirmed that "They've killed President Kennedy." The country seemed to fall apart from that tragic moment on. A spate of reforms, largely triggered by Kennedy's New Frontier inspiration, combined with domestic upheavals, including fiery urban disorders and counterculture rebellions, all coinciding with frustrations of the ever-deepening American involvement in the Vietnamese war, marked a Lyndon Johnson presidency that was simultaneously both productive and destructive, virtually revolutionizing the political climate. Johnson, with the words "let us continue," pushed ahead, taking full advantage of the Kennedy martyrdom, to press for the heart of his predecessor's reform legislation.

Republicans effectively forfeited their chances of regaining the presidency in 1964. Such party traditionalists as Nixon and Rockefeller watched in dismay as Goldwater demonstrated his ability to capitalize on the right-wing euphoria behind him by sweeping the delegates gathered that year in San Francisco's Cow Palace. Enthusiasm soared as his acceptance speech defiantly declared that "extremism in the defense of liberty is no vice," and followed through with the following words: "moderation in the pursuit of justice is no virtue," a statement that many moderates thought gave irresponsible license to the sort of violence that had killed Kennedy and that was becoming ever more a threat to civil society. Given just five minutes by the convention rules to rebut the extremist-sounding Republican platform plank, Rockefeller denounced as "dangerous, irresponsible, and frightening" the new candidate's call to arms. The delegates booed and jeered as New York's governor stood for 16 minutes and "took the abuse of the jackals of the far right," refusing "to be driven from the speaker's platform." Nixon, who had enjoyed Rockefeller's support in 1960, knew, as he later recalled, that Goldwater was going to lose. Recognizing the rapid change in the country's political climate since his own defeat in California, the former vice president abandoned any thoughts of watching the defeat from the sidelines. His 150 campaign stops gave the impression that his zest was nourished by the certainty of Goldwater's defeat. His efforts, he explained, were designed to keep the party's congressional strength at a "respectable level."

The Democratic ticket, meanwhile, confident of victory in the short-term future, stormed the country. More than 60 percent of the popular vote went to Johnson and his running-mate, Senator Hubert Humphrey, reaffirming that the nation was on the brink of the strongest reformist impulse since the New Deal. The presidential election of 1964 confirmed the Democratic emergence as the party most liberal on racial issues, leaving significant numbers of Republicans clinging to the past. The new administration, spurred by the memory of Kennedy's powerful re-election numbers, and the craft of shrewd White House political leadership, delivered significant legislation dealing with poverty, voting rights for previously disenfranchised minorities, housing, and medical care, all under Lyndon Johnson's Great Society.

Southern conservatives reacted sharply to the far-reaching civil rights reforms, which followed the Supreme Court orders to provide racial equality, especially in its *Brown vs. Board of Education* ruling of 1954. Subsequent decisions involving school prayer and voting equality began to turn them away from their post–Civil War and Reconstruction roots. Republicanism finally found respectability in Dixieland.

Two years later, the mid-term elections of 1966 confirmed two things: Americans were indeed doing a political turnaround, and Richard Nixon no longer considered himself retired from national politics. Californians chose Ronald Reagan as the successor to Pat Brown, and a strongly revived conservative coalition swept control of the incoming Congress. As a leading contemporary journalist noted, "the affluence of labor, Negroes, middle-class white liberals, and machine politicians upon which that strength was based is coming apart." With the president becoming obviously bogged down in a war he did not want and did not know how to win, and with mounting turbulence at home, Nixon's appetite for leadership was increasingly replenished. He emerged as a major winner from the party's comeback, working hard for fellow Republicans in 35 states, not only picking up obligations for the future and re-establishing himself, but, at the same time, managing to gather up the disappointed Goldwaterites, reassuring them that their candidate's defeat was largely the fault of his critics. The convergence of the forces most responsible for the shape of postwar American society created the conditions for his resurrection.

His political sophistication had already become most impressive; a seasoned practitioner as he entered his fifties, his vast knowledge of the game and its players had few rivals in the country. He was also, as the *New York Times* reported, "jovial and relaxed and fitted in perfectly with Republican Congressmen . . ." As a public speaker, an increasingly potent part of his talent, he was "a triple threat who touched all the bases."

His contributions included significant attention to the South. There, more than in any other part of the country, he became a true centrist. He delicately balanced sensitivity to traditional attitudes about black-white relationships with the interests of desegregation and compliance with federal law. He called for Republicans and Democrats to campaign on "issues of the future" instead of race. He advised against insisting on segregation while carefully signaling, as he had done before, not only his understanding of the South but his explanation that civil rights was not only a southern issue. In a newspaper column, he warned that "Southern Republicans must not climb aboard the sinking ship of racial injustice."

The 1966 elections offered new encouragement. A Nixon for President Committee, aided by both Mitchell and Garment, was already pushing his candidacy. If such activities were insufficient to point to where the former vice president was headed, his travels during the subsequent months and through much of 1967 were those of a man seeking to build on the foreign policy grounding he had obtained at Dulles's side during the Eisenhower years. Meticulously attentive to details, superbly organized, he maximized his airplane travel time for contemplation and ideas. His knowledge of where he was going, and the problems he was apt to find in those lands, negated any real need for extended briefings on his missions.

Any doubts that remained among specialists who were apprehensive about the breadth of his expertise were at least partly assuaged with the publication in the February 1967 *Foreign Affairs* of Nixon's article, "Asia After Vietnam." It highlighted the future significance of that continent, especially the role of China, foreshadowing a major initiative of his presidency.

The crises of 1967 also eased the way toward his resurrection. The "longest" of the so-called "long hot summers" became notable for headlines about burnings and riots in America's ghettos. Detroit's was the most destructive, but the plague-like restlessness spread to smaller cities and towns. All in all, before the summer of 1967 passed, deaths totaled 225, 4,000 were wounded, and the value of property damaged amounted to some $112 billion. The research division of the Republican National Committee concluded that the summer riots had "starkly dramatized the fact that there is a major crisis in the cities of America," a condition that defied big-government solutions.

Even before the spate of Great Society legislation and the start of ghetto burnings, even before "law and order" became a code, Nixon warned against attempting to force racial equality "in an artificial and unworkable manner," which would cause whatever progress had been achieved to backfire. In terms that appealed to "forgotten" Americans, he deplored the tendency of the Washington bureaucracy, which so often was more representative of the establishment elite, to ignore the problems of middle-class white families who had to labor long hours just to hold on to what they had. They, not the upper-class reformers, would ultimately have to pay the price for social experiments.

Inevitably, in that kind of ready-made climate, Nixon's campaign fund-raising arrangements were also well in place. Conservative Republicans, whatever their misgivings, were encouraged to get behind him as the logical man of the moment, especially after he defended Goldwater from critics who blamed the senator for leading the party to defeat. Their money, not surprisingly, began to move into his campaign war chest. Three fund-raising committees were set up, all in the hands of reliable fat cats. They financed the candidate's activities and enabled him to expand his staff beyond Pat Buchanan, the acerbic, hard-right St. Louis newspaperman who had remained the only full-timer on the payroll. Buchanan, a master of stiletto-like prose, already had the assistance of a New York public relations man, William L. Safire, whose relationship with Nixon dated back to the kitchen debate with Khrushchev.

6

Resurrection

At Christmastime of 1967, Julie Nixon has recalled, her father became more depressed than she had ever seen him before. He had just told her sister Tricia of his decision to skip another run for the presidency, about bucking the long odds. When he discussed his decision in the presence of the girls and Pat, "Mother," his daughter has written, "could not bring herself to urge him to run, but she told him that she would help if he had to make the race." Julie and Tricia were far more enthusiastic than Pat, the long-suffering political wife. "You have to do it for the country," urged Julie, and Tricia added, "If you don't run, Daddy, you really have nothing to live for."

He went off to Key Biscayne, increasingly a vacation retreat with his Cuban-born friend Charles (Bebe) Rebozo, and mulled over the "most important decision" of his life. By the time he returned to New York, his mind was made up, and he had the blessings of all the Nixons, exactly what he instinctively wanted in the first place.

By that point, at least three polls showed Nixon running at least even with Johnson, and certainly ahead of the Republican field. The well-regarded Harris poll gave him a 43-point spread over Rockefeller in California. He also led Michigan's governor George Romney and Ronald Reagan.

Both Reagan and Nixon were drawing from undecided Republicans—and from Democrats as well.

That, indeed, was symptomatic of the Democratic disarray as the nation moved toward the 1968 election, inheriting a difficult history in Southeast Asia. It was Truman, a Democrat, who had first backed the French by spurning the calls of Vietnamese insurgents for help in their struggle against European colonialism. Ike then embraced the cause formally at a conference in Geneva and helped to establish and guarantee the South Vietnamese government under President Ngo Dinh Diem while avoiding intense military involvement. Kennedy, inheriting both the war and the cause as an extension of the goal of containing international Communism to prevent its spread elsewhere in Southeast Asia (like so many falling dominoes), raised the U.S. contribution on the ground to include "advisers" and Special Forces. Johnson's takeover after the Kennedy assassination further escalated the fighting after he used an imaginary enemy "attack" in the Gulf of Tonkin to push the level of American forces toward the half-million mark.

By early 1968, a Democratic moderate, Senator Eugene McCarthy of Minnesota, had already entered the presidential race as an antiwar candidate. That winter, while understood as a defeat for the Vietcong rebels, who counter-attacked after menacing Saigon itself, the three-pronged Tet Offensive (timed to coincide with celebration of the Vietnamese religious Lunar New Year holiday) was immediately reported as further evidence of the enemy's ability to strike at will. Television's most respected news anchor, Walter Cronkite, just back from Vietnam, told his CBS audience on the evening of February 27 that "we are mired in stalemate" and that "the only rational way out . . . will be to negotiate not as victors, but as honorable people who lived up to their pledge to defend democracy and did the best they could." Lyndon Johnson then told his press secretary that if he lost Cronkite, he had lost "Mr. Average Citizen."

Nixon, meanwhile, campaigned cautiously on the subject of the war, neither backing nor opposing the Johnson management. He did, however, according to press reports, suggest that he had "a secret plan" to end the war. But he never did say that, not precisely. One version attributing the comment to him reported an unguarded remark made informally before a small group of reporters. In response to a reporter's question about whether he had a secret plan to end the war, he said, "Yes, I have a *plan* to end the war," without bothering to distinguish between "a plan" and "a secret plan." Clearly, though, he wanted voters to know that he *did* know what to do about Southeast Asia. While campaigning in New Hampshire for the March primary, for example, he asserted, "I say that the American people will be justified in electing new leadership, and I pledge to you that new leadership will end the war and *win the peace in the Pacific.*" To this day, there is no evidence that he actually said he had a *secret* plan, but there is enough reason to believe that he was comfortable having the public believe that he had some sort of scheme. It is fair to concur with the observation that, whatever the nuances at any given moment, his "basic position on how to end the war remained unchanged: send more bombs to Vietnam and more Republicans to Washington." All his comments were *pitched* to a military solution; if there can be peace, he later said, let it be "with honor," whatever that meant. Privately, he doubted that it was even winnable on the battlefields, but, above all, the ultimate solution, he was convinced, must be on terms that were compatible with American political and military interests. Never for a moment did he believe that his rise to the presidency could simply close the curtain on the war in Vietnam.

New Hampshire voted on March 12, and the state's Republicans backed Nixon overwhelmingly, giving him 79 percent while Rockefeller's write-ins came to 11 percent of the total. Nixon had the ability to occupy "the centrist position between Reagan and Rockefeller and thus he would be the beneficiary of the fears on each flank—made Nixon's nomination a virtual certainty . . ." wrote journalist Jules Witcover.

Rockefeller was playing out his own coy game. Nine days after the New Hampshire vote, he announced his withdrawal, although, in late February, he declared himself open to a draft, or a popular demand for his candidacy. At the end of April, to make perfectly clear where he stood, the New York governor re-entered the race, never, however, to become a major player in any of the 12 states with primaries that year.

Nixon, meanwhile, scheduled a Vietnam speech for March 31. Learning that Johnson planned to address the nation that night promptly led him to cancel his own. The president, facing the public with a meager 36 percent approval rating according to the Gallup poll, announced a de-escalation of the war, including suspending the bombing of North Vietnam, a move that eased the way for North Vietnam to negotiate rather than to fight on.

Just as Johnson appeared to have completed his remarks, he looked at a second piece of paper and read, "I shall not seek, and I will not accept, the nomination of my party for another term as President." For a man who loved surprises, he must have considered that one a real coup: Withdrawal was a complete shock.

The calculus of 1968 continued to take unexpected twists and turns. Confusion was then compounded when New York Senator Robert F. Kennedy, the forty-three-year-old former attorney general and younger brother of JFK, joined the competition later in March to unseat the president. To all but the most innocent, it appeared certain that Bobby Kennedy had sensed his opportunity when McCarthy demonstrated surprising strength in that New Hampshire primary, not exactly winning but drawing a remarkably strong 42.4 percent to 49.5 percent for the incumbent president. In Memphis, Tennessee, in early April, the Reverend Dr. Martin Luther King, Jr., there to lead a strike of the city's sanitation workers, was shot and killed. More urban chaos broke, more burnings and lootings. In early June, Bobby Kennedy, after thanking supporters for giving him a victory in the California primary, was shot dead in the kitchen of Los Angeles's Ambassador Hotel. McCarthy, his passion to go on just about drained out of him, allowed his campaign to become a lackluster sleepwalker that frustrated and even infuriated his followers.

State primaries in 1968 had yet to become as widespread as in later years. Of the 12 scheduled, some were already wrapped up by favorite-son candidates. In only three, after New Hampshire, Wisconsin, Nebraska, and Oregon, were there head-to-head contests with the other major candidates, Romney, Rockefeller, and Senator Charles Percy of Illinois. Only Romney was regarded by Nixon as constituting a real threat, and he imploded after confessing to the press that he had been "brainwashed" during a trip to Vietnam. Nixon regarded that collapse as a mixed blessing; it deprived him of the prestige of defeating a strong field.

Several weeks before the Republican convention of 1968, Nixon delivered a radio speech that hailed the coming of new political relationships. FDR's coalition was obsolete, the old alliance of organized labor, minority groups, and Southern Bourbons, progressives, and populists no longer viable. Nixon foresaw a realignment that would tie the new generation, with its post–New Deal values, to traditional Republican doctrines; once they were expressions of the confidence that accompanied the rise of industrial America. Now, in Nixon's words, Washington's role would be "to provide incentives for the private enterprise system to accept some social responsibility. In that context, liberals and conservatives will find themselves coming closer together rather than splitting apart." He called this new constituency, as had Democratic Senator Paul Douglas earlier, the "silent center," a term that later evolved into "silent majority."

Key to success in 1968 was the region of what had been the Solid South, the virtually guaranteed bloc of electoral votes that formed the base of Democratic power for so long. In 1968, Reagan, the best hope of those on the right, and Richard Nixon, hoping to add the region to his coalition without weakening himself elsewhere, were the chief Republican suitors, all in competition with the region's independent, third-party candidate, George Wallace, the former governor of Alabama.

As Nixon was well aware, Wallace was not only competing on his own turf, especially for the votes of white working-class Democrats, but he could also throw the final electoral vote count into the House of Representatives. A staunch segregationist within, one who had promised to preserve "segregation now and forever" and who also emphasized "law-and-order," Wallace could easily thwart Nixon.

At the last moment before the convention, Nixon's other potential competitor for the votes of the old Confederacy, Ronald Reagan, went beyond his favorite-son status in California and turned himself into a valid threat, mustering heavy support from old Goldwater fans and southern delegates.

In the face of that danger, Nixon had no choice except to assure southern committeemen that he understood their view on civil rights. He did not intend to retreat from his support of the Supreme Court's 1954 desegregation decision, but southerners' aversion to busing for desegregating schools was another matter. They were assured about his conviction that forced busing had serious implications for the entire country. Pragmatically, he also met Thurmond's concerns about South Carolina's cotton industry, accepting the need for protection against textiles from Japan and other countries. Southerners, as they reiterated during a meeting in an Atlanta motel on the last day of May, were also concerned about defense, which meant backing the controversial antiballistic missile system, not only to provide assurances against the Russian bear but also to keep the wolf from the door. In addition, Nixon reemphasized his pledge that the South would not be disappointed in his choice of a running mate. It was relatively simple: They would have to take his word but, more than that, recognize that he, unlike Reagan, had the national support to win. That was also sufficient to pull Thurmond away from Wallace.

As if such assurances were not enough, Nixon's grassroots appeals in the South also convinced audiences that he was no more likely than a Wallace, or even a Reagan, to make them swallow desegregation. He did not, in short, think that those states below the Mason-Dixon Line had any greater responsibility than those living up north. The burden was national, not regional. "I don't believe you should use the South as a whipping boy or the North as a whipping boy," he told a friendly crowd in South Carolina," emphasizing that forced busing "can destroy that child." The courts should "interpret the law, and not make the law." For the most part beyond the glare of the national media, such local allies as Thurmond made certain that his words had the maximum effect in the region.

Republicans, sidestepping the opprobrium of race mixing, held their national nominating convention in Miami.

The winner, at least for the top of the ticket, was a forgone conclusion. Having swamped his opposition in the Wisconsin and Oregon primaries, and the most viable remaining threat, Reagan, checkmated in the South, Nixon was a first ballot choice with a plurality of 51 percent out of the 1,333 votes recorded.

His acceptance speech, although heavily exploitative of the national concern with domestic unease by stressing the "law-and-order" theme, foreshadowed his presidential efforts to achieve a new majority. He represented the "forgotten Americans—the non-shouters, the non-demonstrators," the dynamos of the "American dream," working together to carry forth the "greatest engine of progress ever developed in the history of man—American private enterprise."

Having blocked Reagan, and while never forgiving the former actor for turning his non-candidacy into a real challenge, Nixon made good on his wooing of the South by delivering on the rest of his promise to Thurmond. A relative unknown, Spiro Agnew, Nixon's vice presidential choice, beat out a list of far more imposing contenders. As a novice politician who had only recently made it to Maryland's governorship, Agnew was in line with Nixon's seeming preference to, as one of his aides put it, "ethnic types." Nixon later instructed his chief of staff, "don't think in terms of old-line ethnics, go for Poles, Italians, Irish, must learn to understand Silent Majority. . . . don't go for Jews & Blacks"—in other words, the two traditionally outside groups that were both anathema to the components of Nixon's contemplated "new majority." Nixon thereby wooed the white backlash that grew out of the civil rights reforms of the past two decades.

Agnew was less subtle. His ethnicity was clearly in tune with "displaced" whites, especially those who had to "sweat" for a living. The son of Greek immigrants, rough hewn as he seemed to many, Agnew carried two other important credentials: At the state house in Annapolis, he had won plaudits with some for facing down some 100 middle-class black leaders from Baltimore by suggesting that they shared responsibility for the city's riots; and, until Rockefeller unexpectedly took himself out of the running, Agnew's public endorsement of the New Yorker gave him the aura of a moderate. Some people may also have considered him as somewhat of a liberal because he had won the governorship by defeating a hard-shell right winger.

A border state man to boot, Agnew was also Nixon's answer to Wallace. Whatever remained of the potency of Alabama's governor, however, was later destroyed by his unfortunate choice of "the bomber," General Curtis E. LeMay, as his running mate. Introduced at a press conference, the general torpedoed the Wallace-LeMay ticket single handedly by his almost rhapsodic denunciation of "a phobia about nuclear weapons."

By building on the process that had gone before, stretching all the way from the Dixiecrat revolt against Truman in 1948, to the "Eisencrats" of the 1950s, and the powerful support given by the region to Goldwater in 1964, Nixon's campaign represented a coming of age. Thirty-six years after Roosevelt's first election, the elements of a watershed were in place. For those who had had their fill of power-laden White Houses, Nixon offered the prospect of an administration that, like Eisenhower's, would filter policies through greater reliance on his cabinet. Shrewdly, in several ways, Nixon had seized on the substantial divisions that marked postwar American politics.

The Democrats, however, as had been their pattern of late, continued to destroy themselves. Their convention at Chicago, three weeks after the GOP had chosen the Nixon-Agnew ticket, turned into an unmitigated disaster, fully revealed in all its chaotic detail for television audiences everywhere. Radicals, determined to disrupt the proceedings, found Mayor Richard Daley's police all too eager to cooperate in meeting uninhibited resistance both to authority and conventional views of morality by turning the challenge into their own version of class warfare. Within the hall, as many Democrats attempted to go through the proceedings as though the eyes of the nation were not riveted on the streets, Senator Abraham Ribicoff's attempt to turn their attention to what was happening "to our children" on the streets drew obscenities from the mayor that were read by lip readers everywhere. A later commission characterized the law enforcement efforts as a "police riot," but two out of every three Americans approved of the police actions. Strongly behind Mayor Daley, the confrontation highlighted the realities of American socioeconomic lines. By the time the Democrats wound up their work in Chicago by nominating Vice President Hubert Humphrey and Senator Edwin Muskie of Maine as his running mate, conventional wisdom questioned whether the prize was worth having.

In reality, however, the outcome was far from settled. As Nixon and Humphrey fought each other until America voted on November 5, the outcome clearly turned on the war in Vietnam. Humphrey, meeting resistance from the die-hard McCarthy peace wing of the party, did not soften them until the end of September, when he joined the call to de-escalate the war. Nixon resisted Humphrey's challenges to debate; determined to face the electorate as the wise statesman, one who also had the endorsement of the terminally ill Dwight Eisenhower, he talked to the nation via radio in mid-October about the "eventual" need for "conversations with the leaders of Communist China" because there "is no place on this small planet for a billion of its most able people to live in angry isolation." As Nixon wrote to his chief of staff, Bob Haldeman, a year later, the Wallace factor, with polls showing that the Alabaman was "*drawing approximately two votes from Nixon for every one that he drew from Humphrey*" still made the probable final result too close so that "we could take nothing for granted." Wallace's ability to draw support from the segregationist White Citizens' Councils and the Ku Klux Klan was a significant factor.

The full dimension of Nixon's role has long since become clear—playing a game of life-and-death poker in an eleventh-hour maneuver of swinging a close presidential election. After all considerations and evidence have been weighed, it is clear that Nixon, in an effort to keep things hot on the battlefield for a few more weeks, was knowingly risking even more lives, 30,000 of which had already been lost in the Vietnamese jungles and rice paddies. The American people knew nothing about the behind-the-scenes maneuvering as they prepared to vote on November 5.

Central to that scenario was the glamorous and well-connected Chinese widow of World War II Flying Tiger hero General Claire Chennault, Anna Chennault, together with the off-stage presence of Henry Kissinger, Nelson Rockefeller's foreign policy adviser. Kissinger, playing both sides with a series of informative phone calls, supplied the provocative information, Nixon the scheme, and the so-called "Dragon Lady" (the co-chair with Mamie Eisenhower of Republican Women for Nixon, and a $250,000 fund-raiser for the Nixon campaign) the means, all to head off a pre-election cease-fire. How could such a last-minute dramatic breakthrough not throw the victory to Humphrey? Keeping Nixon informed, and confirming Kissinger's information, was Bryce Harlow, an Eisenhower administration veteran. Harlow, in turn, was in touch with a friend in the Johnson White House. After hearing from Kissinger that things were about to happen in Paris and anticipating something sensational that could well decide the election, John Mitchell met with Madame

The President and his key aides, Henry Kissinger, John Ehrlichman, and H. R. Haldeman, in the Oval Office © NLRNS/National Archives

Chennault in Nixon's New York apartment. He asked her to serve as "his channel" to South Vietnamese President Nguyen Van Thieu.

The crucial development that fall followed a signal from the Communist government in Hanoi that the North Vietnamese would consider participating in peace talks in Paris. Soviet fear that a Johnson defeat might produce stronger anti-Communist diplomacy and fewer favorable terms than the North could get while Democrats were still in power evidently encouraged the move. Harlow relayed such developments to Nixon, who, in turn, did not trust Johnson's ability to resist the kind of political coup that would very likely enable Humphrey to win. It little mattered that acceptance did not make tactical sense to the South Vietnamese. Their power was totally dependent on the Americans, who already had 550,000 soldiers in the country. Nixon, however, the perpetual worrier as well as analyst, was not one to leave things to chance. He secretly urged the South Vietnamese leader to "hold on."

Playing his poker hand, he issued a public statement with assurances of support for Johnson's diplomacy. The president, not a bad card player himself, immediately scorned the move as a ploy designed to suggest that Nixon was only interested in playing politics with the campaign, which was given more substance by his criticism of Humphrey for sabotaging the negotiations. Johnson, not surprised by anything Nixon might do, grumbled that he was, after all, "a man who distorts the history of his time." Kissinger, seeing Nixon up close for the first time, understood that he was determined to run foreign policy from the White House rather than the State Department.

In a conference call to Humphrey, Nixon, and Wallace just before publicly announcing that he would suspend bombing North Vietnam as of November 1, Johnson explained that there were some obstacles to be overcome and pointedly said, "*I know that none of you candidates are aware of it or responsible for it.*" Nixon, true to his tactics, immediately assumed the role of a loyal opponent, vowing at a New York Madison Square Garden rally, that neither he nor Agnew "will say anything that might destroy the chance to have peace." Johnson, meanwhile, incorrectly but with logic on his side, assumed that delays in getting an agreement to pin down the start of the talks were due to interventions by Nixon's people.

Nevertheless, his announcement of October 31 did give Humphrey an immediate boost in the polls. His numbers jumped from a two-point deficit to a slight lead. But then, Thieu quickly slammed the door on that prospect, acting as much for his own interests as Nixon's, restoring the Republican challenger's front-runner status. With or without outside help, the South Vietnamese president had concluded that his bargaining hand would be strengthened by having a Republican in the White House. Nixon, acting as an innocent, publicly derided Johnson's inability to jump-start the peace talks. If elected, he even pledged, he would, if the president "would deem [it] helpful . . . go to Paris or to Saigon in order to get the negotiations off dead center"—shades of Ike's promise to "go to Korea" back in 1952.

Through FBI and CIA wiretaps on Thieu and having Chennault under surveillance, Johnson knew all about her contacts. The information, however, could not be revealed (and Humphrey bitterly kept it to himself) without admitting spying on America's South Vietnamese clients. Even if Thieu had acted without influence, Nixon had indulged in the dirtiest of dirty tricks. The stakes could not have been higher; the future of the U. S. commitment and the prospects for Southeast Asia all hung on it, to say nothing of the additional cost of lives caused by a delay. Johnson thought Nixon was guilty of "treason," his anger even compelling him to return to active campaigning for Humphrey after having been notably cool about the prospects of his potential successor. Johnson also rejected making any public accusation that Nixon had manipulated foreign negotiations, a move that could have provoked a constitutional crisis by opening Nixon to possible indictment and prosecution. In any event, even if he had been exonerated, it could have crippled his presidency. As it turned out, Nixon was indebted to Thieu, whether or not he had to be.

After Nixon had been safely elected, his camp pushed the same Madame Chennault, by her own account, *to help get peace talks back on track*—better to have it over with before his own inauguration. On election day, Nixon called Johnson and "categorically denied any connection or knowledge" of the affair, which brought guffaws from staffers who overhead their conversation. Later confronted during an interview about Chennault's role, he treated the whole thing dismissively. She was merely "a self-promoter."

The electorate split three ways on November 5. Nixon was the popular choice with 43.4 percent, followed by Humphrey's 42.7. Wallace, many of whose supporters defected from what they feared would be a "wasted vote," wound up with 13.5 percent, a number that clearly reflected the apparent futility of voting for the candidate of a minor party, the American Independence Party. A final tally of the Electoral College, while more decisive, offered a clearer warning for the winner: 301 for Nixon, 191 for Humphrey, and 46 for Wallace, all from five of the former Confederate States of America. As telling, perhaps, despite organized labor's efforts to keep their workers in line and his third-party candidacy, the Alabama governor received some 15 to 18 percent of union members across the country. Humphrey, at the same time, drew just 35 percent of the white votes.

What remained of Humphrey's base constituency was prophetic, confirming the thinness of the old New Deal majority. Not only did Nixon sweep non-minority voters, but he most attracted those well-educated and upwardly mobile citizens of affluent suburbs, heavily Protestant and from the South. Their great priorities, aside from prosperity, were maintaining law and order and solving the war in Vietnam. Nobody—least of all Nixon, who took history seriously—could have missed the reality that he was about to inherit the leadership, as one friend put it, "of a divided government in a deeply divided country." Making that divide more emphatic was continued Democratic control over both houses of the Ninety-first Congress, by 243 to 192 in the House and 58 to 42 in the Senate. Not since 1848 had a new president been elected without enabling his party to win control of either chamber on Capitol Hill.

Little wonder, then, that he took his post-election theme from the words "Bring Us Together Again," which appeared on a sign held aloft by a young girl during the campaign. That would be the "great objective of this administration at the outset, to bring the American people together. This will be an open administration, open to new ideas, open to men and women of both parties, open to the critics as well as those who support us. . . . We want to bring America together."

7

A Governing Center

From the moment of his election as the thirty-seventh president, Richard Nixon's recovery from political oblivion was fulfilled; the options before him presented an array of short- and long-term objectives. The first, normal and within the purview of any political leader, was to refine his administration's ability to govern. The outcome, as Nixon envisioned, would be a reconfiguration of the heart of American political power, one that would create a governing center. His updated coalition would be a "new majority."

In addition to the traditional partisan alignments, Nixon had to respond to the increasingly popular appeals of George C. Wallace. The Alabama governor, at times fiery, crude, and demagogic, skillfully exploited the resentments that created tensions between poor whites and minorities. His supporters cheered far more wildly attacks on radicals and antiwar demonstrators than *for* programs aimed at relieving poverty and other economic inequities. Those dissidents, Nixon later argued, could potentially cripple the country internationally as well as domestically; such diplomacy as negotiating an end to the war in Vietnam and détente with the People's Republic of China and the Soviet Union would become politically impossible.

Nixon's incoming administration had to overcome two other obstacles: Finding how to end the fighting, which had already taken some 30,000 American lives, and stabilizing the economy and social order in a way that would preserve the dreams of the "forgotten Americans."

The remote and often incomprehensible war had already engaged four presidents. Early on, Harry Truman backed the French by spurning the calls of Vietnamese for help in their struggle against European colonialism. His successor, Dwight D. Eisenhower, embraced the imperial cause openly at a conference in Geneva and helped to establish and guarantee the survival of the South Vietnamese government under President Ngo Dinh Diem while avoiding overt military involvement. Inheriting both the war and its goal as part of the cold-war containment of Communism, Kennedy acted to help avoid the enemy cause's spread elsewhere in Southeast Asia, the potential result of what was often described as the danger of "falling dominoes." His "new frontier" administration raised the U.S. manpower contribution to include "advisers" and Special Forces. Lyndon Johnson's inheritance after Kennedy's assassination led to his further escalation of the fighting. His most fateful decision included using a shadowy enemy "attack" in the Gulf of Tonkin to push the troop level to the half-million mark. He left the White House under vehement antiwar protests and so frustrated in his pursuit of the elusive victory that, in 1968, he took himself out of the campaign for re-election.

It was left to Nixon to suggest that he had somewhat of a "peace" plan. Continuing the reversal that began to manifest itself after Johnson's final year, especially after the North Vietnamese Tet offensive, he turned to a strategy that involved gradual assumption of the fighting by indigenous forces, what the administration called "Vietnamization," to avoid having to suffer defeat and to secure his stated goal of "peace with honor."

Nixon's rise to power brought hopes for a new direction. Eighty-two percent of Americans, according to one public opinion poll released that January, were confident that he really wanted to end the war soon, which did nothing to assuage antiwar radicals, who helped turn his inaugural into an especially tumultuous event. "Crazies," the most extreme militants, planted themselves along the parade route, tossing smoke bombs, rocks, bottles, and obscenities at the limousine that carried Nixon and the new First Lady. Protesters repeatedly chanted "Four more years of death!"

Senator Barry Goldwater described the inaugural celebrations as "an obscene Roman holiday. We were at war." But Nixon, to his surprise, learned from a *Washington Star* editorial, there were no arrests. "Why not?" he wanted to know from John Ehrlichman. "I think an opportunity was missed when people would have suggested strong action."

His speech, however, emphasized a different tone. He reached out to both the young and the disaffected, reminding them that "we are caught in a war, wanting peace. We are torn by division, wanting unity." Then, quixotically, he went on, "we need an answer of the spirit. And to find that answer, we need only look within ourselves. . . . To lower our voices would be a simple thing. In these difficult years, America has suffered from a fever of words; from inflated rhetoric that promises more than it can deliver; from angry rhetoric that fans discontents into hatreds; from bombastic rhetoric that postures instead of persuading. We cannot learn from one another until we stop shouting at one another—until we speak quietly enough so that our words can be heard as well as our voices."

His final passage was the most memorable. "We have endured a long night of the American spirit," he said. "But as our eyes catch the dimness of the first rays of dawn, let us not curse the remaining dark. Let us gather the light."

Characteristically, Nixon at his inauguration was not only concerned with performing impeccably (a favorite word) but, perhaps even more, with having the world appreciate that he was doing an impeccable job. Even before his swearing-in, he wanted the country to recognize the diligence with which he had selected the incoming cabinet; the arrival of the first Republican in the White House since Eisenhower also implied a reduced federal bureaucracy, and, as with Ike in 1953, an efficient solution for an increasingly unpopular war. Eisenhower himself was passing from the scene; within 48 hours after Nixon visited him at Walter Reed Army Hospital, the thirty-fourth president was dead, emphasizing, even in the early hours of his own presidency, that Nixon was his own man, liberated from the past.

Most assuredly, Nixon was not Eisenhower. The old soldier commanded his administration as a chairman of the board, pulling the strings from behind the scene. Weeks before the inaugural, Nixon's introduction of the incoming cabinet was staged as a great video extravaganza. He wanted "new men with new ideas," not a cabinet of "yes-men," but, ideally, an open, democratic administration. "Get some of the non-elite businessmen," he demanded at one point. "They produce. They are with us." "Increasingly," his daughter Julie has written, "loyalty was demanded of all, not judgment."

Henry Kissinger, the child of a family that fled from Germany in time to escape the Holocaust and who served in U.S. military intelligence in World War II, came to Nixon by way of Harvard and Nelson Rockefeller. Kissinger, clearly, as attested to by subordinates and peers, was blatantly political and could be personally brutal. During the 1968 elections, he had established a reputation for playing both sides of the street. He and Nixon, presumably allied, became "rivals, paranoid and insecure, deceitful and manipulative, ruthless and strangely vulnerable," in the words of historian Robert Dallek.

The real power center basically reached out only as far as the newly-appointed adviser for National Security Affairs, Kissinger, and included H. R. (Bob) Haldeman, a graduate of the University of Southern California and a successful West Coast advertising man, as chief of staff, along with Ehrlichman, who came to head what Nixon called the Domestic Affairs Council. That was precisely where the president wanted to position foreign policy initiatives, within the White House along with Haldeman and Ehrlichman and not with "elitist" state department types; having Bill Rogers at their head as secretary suited him fine.

As one critic later noted, Nixon "built a bureaucracy to control the bureaucracy," and the White House staff mushroomed instead of shrank. Nixon later explained that putting his "stamp on the federal bureaucracy as quickly and as firmly as we possibly could" was "one of our most important tasks," and that included the need to "Republicanize" the executive departments and agencies.

At the heart of the administration was the president himself—relishing his authority to do as he pleased, whatever he pleased, whether by risking ridicule by outfitting the White House Secret Service detail in the elaborate ceremonial regalia of Swiss guards or by firing up the logs in his fireplace, whatever the outdoor temperature or the season and whether he was in the White House or at his Maryland retreat. The solitude-seeking president sought excuses to avoid large gatherings and was clearly uncomfortable with people and wary of strangers. He had, in some ways, a most unlikely political persona, better suited, some thought, for the academic world than a political clubhouse.

His ruminations often found their way onto his handy yellow legal pad. At one point, reviewing on paper his administration's score so far, he decided that he had reestablished dignity in the White House but was falling into the danger of looking like he was being "*managed* by planners." He wasn't sure where he stood, or where he ought to go or, for that matter, what would be the force that *he* could lead. If he formed a new party, would it be conservative or would it be liberal? His "major role," he decided at one point, "is moral leadership. I cannot exercise this adequately unless I speak out more often & more eloquently." What he really needed, he decided, was "for more stimulating people to talk to." Privacy was indeed a welcome escape. He was, after all, *the president*. His desires were quickly and efficiently targeted to the appropriate aides throughout the White House by "ticklers," the crisp memoranda that flowed from Haldeman's desk. To hear insiders tell it, they functioned with machine precision.

His commands were their gospel. Other administrations have been described as insular empires, there to execute in behalf of the presidency, their only and highest mission and the essence of executive office efficiency. The office of chief of staff, first formally created during the Eisenhower presidency, was strengthened during Nixon's.

Most presidents, especially those eager to consolidate power, are the principal shapers of the climate within the White House. Nixon, given his own disposition, and some very real reasons for feeling besieged, clearly set the tone of his administration. His men, predictably, were almost uniformly eager, ambitious, and in awe of their responsibility to protect the president and further his interests.

Throughout Nixon's presidency and later, in memoirs and taped conversations, much evidence from his White House years confirmed the importance of their mission to safeguard their boss over any other need, a step toward what was later described as a "unitary executive."

* * *

Nixon "did not bleed for the poor," his top economic adviser explained, but neither was he about to "send them into the streets." His devotion to the "free market" did not blind him from the realization that it also created victims. His populism blended with innate conservatism and resembled what came to be popularly known as "traditional values." He understood that helping the underclasses depended on the patience of the middle classes, an inherent source of tension that would be further strained if they abused the intent and rejected middle-class standards.

The new, post–Great Depression, postwar generation—the so-called baby boomers—was composed of "rugged individualists" in the American tradition. In large part, they were neither the direct beneficiaries of FDR's New Deal programs nor of the compensations designed for World War II veterans. They wanted to believe that they had made it on their own and thought everyone else could do the same. That was, after all, the essence of the American Dream.

That's where Patrick Daniel Moynihan came in. Moynihan, a Democrat and also a Harvard professor as well as a former assistant in the Kennedy and Johnson labor departments, was an indulgence. The forty-two-year-old intellectual was stimulating and exciting to have around; without him, the White House could be pretty lonely and a grim sort of privacy.

Nixon understood Moynihan. His kind of liberalism verged on the classical and could pass for traditional conservatism. He was the Irish kid from Manhattan's Hell's Kitchen neighborhood whose mother ran a saloon on Forty-second Street. He put in time as a stevedore and saw workers from up close. But he had also made good;

he became an Ivy Leaguer and had played in the big leagues with the intellectuals. He was impatient with theorists who wanted to make over the world. He saw some of them firsthand at an East Side Democratic club, where gentleman reformers conjured up utopian designs but did not care about real workers.

He told Nixon that since he was a conservative, he had a chance to emulate British Tories and reach down to do something for the lower classes. Moynihan understood how Disraeli had taken hold of the social agenda, so Nixon would do well to read about Disraeli's life. The president was impressed. He quoted the English statesman about educational reform in public. It was notable, he thought, that Disraeli, "born a Jew" and "in trouble during youth," became the "ablest practical politician of the late 1800's in Britain." He was even a novelist and a poet. That's what we need, said Nixon, "a little more poetry." The Disraeli analogy was a fine way to convince Nixon that one could be socially concerned and conservative at the same time.

Nixon's appeal for Moynihan is understandable. He was less dense than the liberals Moynihan had had to buck in Johnson's Labor Department and in the civil rights movement. Under the Democrats, Moynihan's ideas had drawn blanks. He tried to convince his colleagues that civil rights legislation alone was not going to fill the stomachs of the poor. The underclass needed jobs, and no one else around Johnson believed more strongly that the most effective thing that could be done to save blacks from welfare and their own plight was to put them to work; Nixon really liked that about Moynihan. He also thought that employment was the first priority. Without money, all else would fail.

Three days after the inauguration, on January 23, Nixon issued an executive order establishing a Council of Urban

Affairs (later, the Urban Affairs Council), with Moynihan at its head as a presidential assistant. His mandate, the new administration made clear, was to make specific recommendations in the area of population growth and family planning, and to coordinate his missions with the Department of Health, Education and Welfare.

Moynihan or no Moynihan, Nixon's political instincts ruled out decimating the Kennedy-Johnson social programs. Neither then nor later, whatever the changing course of his administration, did he think of himself as indifferent toward society's disadvantaged. "We were not zealots," Nixon himself later explained; "we were not trying to return to a Calvin Coolidge era." He had hoped to remain in office long enough to do something about matters that government in America had scanted, becoming, in fact, enough of an enigma, as conservative a Republican as he was, to even be thought of as the "last liberal" president of the twentieth century, one who began to "preside over a more rapid evolution toward planning than any other President since FDR." At his initial meeting with the Republican congressional leadership, he emphasized his intent to move "decisively and differently" from the ways of his predecessors. He was the one who should be recognized as "the man in charge—a man who must be the Chief Executive." In the first days of his first February in office he sneered at a press report that his presidency was "a government by committee" and wanted it known widely that "RN [as he often referred to himself] provides every positive direction leadership to the Cabinet committees . . ."

From the start, "RN" appreciated the potential leverage of a strong political base, and he aimed to create a new majority from among the elements of the electorate not attached to any dominant elite sector. His populist instincts, mostly evident early on from the days of his

Checkers speech, were further honed by the upheavals of the sixties. He learned to capitalize on the resentments of those who felt left behind.

Nixon never doubted that men were instinctively selfish. His was a Hobbesian world, "solitary, poor, nasty, brutish, and short." Leadership, to be effective, had to save man from himself. That was what society was all about. But all too often, and Nixon had seen it over and over again, the "leadership class," so empowered, got its privileges for no better reason than the accident of birth and the advantages of wealth.

From the outset, Nixon exerted his authority over policies, minor and major, overseeing every detail, every move of personnel, with sufficient attention to detail to raise questions about his proximity to all aspects of the administration. He was the dynamic force, inseparable from all that was going on. Nixon had a passion for tactics, and, as a tactician, he was a warrior. "You see," he pointed out to speechwriter Safire, "the press is the enemy. . . . I want more one-liners. We want to help our friends who help themselves, and not support those who help our enemies."

He also fully appreciated how he had to battle the odds. By the time he reached the presidency, he had long assumed foreign policy as his primary interest. War had broken Truman, empowered Eisenhower, dominated Kennedy, and brought Johnson to despair and resignation. Nixon had already seen more of the world than most American politicians. Nothing he had seen changed his mind about the inherent threats of the Marxist impulse. If the non-socialist world relaxed, the appeal of the materialistic analysis, promoted by force and the self-interest of the Communist leadership class, would simply spread, choking the lifelines of free commerce. And, of course, the persistence of poverty haunted the globe and the applications of American interests. Nixon, instead of dismissing the problem as one to be handled by the free market, feared that the Russians would forever exploit its existence.

"If the United States withdraws into a new isolation," he warned long after his White House years were over, "there is no other power that shares our values and possesses the resources and the will to take our place. At the same time, we can be sure that another power hostile to our values and interests, the Soviet Union, will do so." Nations, in their predatory instincts, were as aggressive as individuals, no more warranting trust because of special virtues. Those having systems without similar spiritual and cultural ethics, especially belief in individual progress, were the ones that most needed watching. Any changes would be illusory, evocative of great hope, but, alas, tactical and temporary; power and the preservation of socialism would continue as the long-term self-interest.

The concept of a "foreign policy" president had long been a cliché of American political leadership, the product of a federal system in which those in the Oval Office had the broadest constitutional responsibility and the greatest range of options. For a variety of reasons other than law, resistance to strong chief executives was also weakest when executives dealt with the rest of the world. The mastery of foreign policy, valid or otherwise, came with the oath of office. But, as he well knew, those major responsibilities, foreign and domestic, were inseparable.

* * *

The first White House news summary shown to him detailed an image of a national capital that, nine months after the extensive damage from the rioting and fires that followed the murder of Dr. Martin Luther King, Jr., was a "city of fear and crime." In just one 30-hour period, "six men died in the Washington area in three double killings," and "two of the dead men were agents of the

Federal Bureau of Investigation." "We are going to make a major effort to reduce crime in [the] nation—starting with D.C.," the new president scribbled on the page. To Ehrlichman, he directed that it was "of highest priority to do something meaningful on D.C. crime *now*." All the way from the streets of America to the jungles of Vietnam, it was clear that Nixon had simply inherited Lyndon Johnson's problems. Any "new" politics, noted one professional analyst, was less likely to be the politics "of the beard and the sandal" than the politics of "the gray flannel suit, of Nixon's pragmatic center." Nixon, moreover, was determined to avoid his predecessor's fate. "I have the *will* in spades," he wrote to Henry Kissinger, realizing also that it was not only the specter of a failed Johnson but the reality of a very viable George Wallace, whose followers railed at campus disruptions, drugs, and pornography. At the Justice Department, meanwhile, the newcomers stashed away blank executive orders for the possible declaration of martial law in any affected city.

Ever since the 1960s, and in the face of liberal Supreme Court decisions, the words "law and order" had become code terminology for not only fear of crime but also of racial conflict. A nation that had largely discarded the death penalty underwent an abrupt reversal with a majority suddenly ready to embrace capital punishment. Courts were too lenient; street crimes had become the number one concern in communities all over the country, with some 80 percent of the public fearing a breakdown of the legal system. A conservative mayoral candidate in New York City disparaged "limousine liberals." Sam Yorty became mayor of Los Angeles by exploiting racial divisions. Frank Rizzo, a strong law-and-order man, and an Italian of great appeal to Philadelphia's ethnic whites, became mayor with the strong backing and financial support of Nixon's friend, publishing magnate Walter Annenberg. Nelson

Rockefeller, the Empire State's icon of liberal Republican-ism, initiated draconian drug enforcement laws. Demonstrations against court-ordered busing for desegregation also flared in New York City and Boston. Democrats, of course, the creators of the Warren Court and "bleeding heart" worriers about the rights of the poor and minorities, were caught up on the losing end of the issue. No opponent who governed during that period, and certainly not Nixon, could fail to miss the sources of "political juice."

The fact is that, whatever the sociological components, order had to be first established at home, or at least a credible effort had to be made. The national capital itself, within federal jurisdiction, was the best place to begin. As the "crime clock" of the *Washington Daily News* showed, Nixon noted, "some action on the crime front is imperative at an early point. I feel the need to do something more dramatic than simply repeating the need for more police, more courts, more public defenders," Nixon informed John Mitchell, his attorney general. "Possibly we have to bring in some law enforcement officials from other areas of the government—U.S. marshals, Secret Service, FBI, anything you may think of to shore up the District crime force so that we can stop this escalation of crime in the nation's capital." Without solving those problems and ending the quagmire in Vietnam, his would be a one-term presidency.

Attorney General Mitchell appealed for individual citizens to contribute to raise funds for volunteer action to fight crime, and the administration lost little time getting on record with omnibus law-and-order recommendations, also reporting that the Department of Housing and Urban Development had approved a $29.7 million neighborhood development plan for the devastated district, with an immediate $1 million in interim funds to be made available. In striking hard to make a national point against crime, the administration also called for greater home rule for the city and for more stringent enforcement of the federal anti-narcotics law enacted in 1966. On June 26, Mitchell made another appeal on behalf of the administration. Testifying on Capitol Hill, he opposed the renewal of the Voting Rights Act of 1965, which was one of the Johnson administration's most effective contributions to the battle for equality. Mitchell's testimony made a point that was consistent with Nixon's national "southern strategy"—or, as some observers thought, "suburban strategy"—and also showed the eagerness to tackle juicier domestic issues.

His opposition to busing, the calls for law and order, the crafting of a District of Columbia crime bill, together with a no-knock provision that outraged civil libertarians, were also inseparable from his efforts to diffuse the Wallace threat. In that matter, as in every other one dealing with the question of civil rights and attempts to alleviate the inequities of discrimination, Nixon's approach was strictly one of political expediency, as on most domestic issues. Only foreign policy, namely, America's relationships to the rest of the world, fired him emotionally and intellectually.

One of Mitchell's attorneys, John Dean, was pushed up from Justice to the White House to become counsel to the president. It is redundant to describe any of these men as "ambitious" because of the rarity of finding one who was not.

Almost from the outset of the administration, ultimately to figure as significantly as did Dean in the annals of Nixon's presidency, were the beginnings of what later became known as the Plumbers. Begun as a political intelligence arm of an increasingly insular White House, the unit functioned, ironically, apart from the established federal security agencies as well as the Republican Party. Set up by Ehrlichman and starting out with a former New York City cop, John Caulfield, the extra-legal ad hoc group attracted ex-CIA and FBI agents and went to work targeting

Nixon's political opposition as traitorous and disloyal—a clandestine apparatus that destroyed its creators. As historian Keith Olson has noted, since the start of his presidency, Nixon had "routinely and repeatedly employed illegal activities within the executive branch of the federal government . . . all related to information about opponents and concern about information leaks in the context of foreign policies and opposition to those policies."

* * *

Yet, at the same time, paradoxically, one would have to go back to Theodore Roosevelt's time to find a Republican presidency more actively engaged in progressive domestic reform. Nixon's record in that area has been understood mostly in retrospect and, even then, considered as somewhat incongruous. He successfully avoided the appearance of liberalism while wooing conservatives, especially southerners. From the outset of the administration, machinery was already in place to take on such issues as civil rights, environmental legislation, and social services, if only, as has been pointed out, for politically pragmatic reasons.

Shrewdly, Nixon *simultaneously placed himself against federal activism and, paradoxically, as an agent of reform.* In a long memorandum to the president, Ehrlichman explained that "some non-conservative initiatives [have been] deliberately designed to furnish some zigs to go with our conservative zags in the same way we have included Moynihans with our Dents [South Carolina's Republican chairman] rather than trying to recruit only those non-existent middle-of-the-roaders."

A review of Nixon's legislative policies may reasonably agree, as has been done, that they represented an astute balancing act, one that maneuvered between reluctance to shock the system by abruptly attempting to cancel recent reforms and signaling to conservatives, especially southern supporters, that he thought Democrats forced federal policies down the throats of old-fashioned states' righters. Not surprisingly, all this went under the label of "New Federalism" with its capstone program emerging as a process of revenue sharing to empower the states to use federal blocs of money at their local discretion. Other results included a Clean Air Act, which accelerated the conversion by public utilities from high-sulfur coal to low-sulfur oil. Environmentalists hailed it as a major contribution in the effort to control air pollution. Other measures, generally in a progressive direction, were enhanced Social Security benefits, tax reform, and even continued funding for the Office of Economic Opportunity, under the direction of a thirty-six-year-old Republican from Illinois, Donald Rumsfeld.

Nixon emerged from all this, according to one thorough student, as "a conservative man of liberal views, not too liberal and not too conservative—judiciously expanding the reach of government to benefit his constituents and solve the nation's problems." As his adviser for domestic affairs, Ehrlichman assured him, "Very few initiatives will be truly in the center. They will fall on one side or the other. Our domestic policy job . . . [is] to insure some *balance*. As we can, consistent with the Social Issue concept, we will try to co-opt the opposition's issues . . . if the political cost is not too great."

He sponsored important environmental legislation but not at the expense of jobs. He proposed welfare reform in the form of reverse tax payments to provide a guaranteed income for the poor who worked, but that required work of poor recipients who did not (Family Assistance Plan or FAP). Designed to replace the more than three-decade-old New Deal system of Aid to Families With Dependent Children that had come under widespread criticism for abuse with a system of "work-fare," it was aimed at those at the bottom of the economy. To protect workers, he sponsored legislation to upgrade safety in the workplace. To help both working-class and middle-income voters, he presided over an expanded social security system. The "zigs and zags" of policy gave the appearance of ideological confusion, enigmatic to those trying to fathom conventional ideological definitions. Politics provided the coherence, and because politics was the point, Nixon cared more about the symbolism of his program—how it played in Peoria—than in actually passing it. The cost was too great, he felt, but a "big play" had to be made for it, and then it had to be seen as being killed by the Democrats.

He later acknowledged that he "knew that wasn't going to happen," but such moves were necessary to be "politically viable," in order to be in office, in order to carry forward "progressive actions," even if at the price of taking positions that annoyed the liberals.

He held no illusions, however, about black equality. In a discussion with Ehrlichman on April 28, 1969, Nixon pointed out that "you have to face the fact that the *whole* problem is really the blacks. The key is to devise a system that recognizes this while not appearing to." Then, as though to reinforce his point with a bit of genetics, he noted that blacks have "never in history" created an "adequate nation," and only Liberia, "which we built," is the part of Africa that is not "hopeless."

Failure to achieve the kind of welfare reform involved in the Family Assistance Plan was the administration's most significant domestic loss, but it made the point: Welfare reform, after much contention over the assistance program carried over from the New Deal, did not fail because of Nixon's failures. The president himself was quick to sign on to Moynihan's point about a welfare bureaucracy of social workers fighting to maintain the status quo, and, after all, it was a Democratic Congress that had caused the death of the Family Assistance Plan.

* * *

Winning reelection is every bit as compelling a need as is the desire to get there in the first place. The original victory is often a test of political skill; the second, a measure of leadership, the two most vital ingredients of a public career. In that sense, Richard Nixon was a *conventional* politician; if cunning was prerequisite for strength, he was also a *strong* one. Chief executives who exercised their constitutional prerogatives to the hilt were far more likely to win the respect of political scientists and historians, especially as American power became more internationalized during the twentieth century. Hardly anyone who ascended to the White House was oblivious of that reality, and Richard Nixon, intelligent, proud, and ready to win at all costs, was prepared for the role, as he confirmed during a 1988 interview, which also left little doubt that Wallace was much on his mind.

What happened to the process of desegregating America's public schools in fulfillment of the Supreme Court's 1954 landmark decision is a valid if little recognized example. It will forever remain remarkable that, without serious confrontation and bold headlines, the Nixon administration, with the valuable help of Labor Secretary Shultz, achieved the effective desegregation of the old dual system of education. It is sobering to recall that as recently as 1969, 68 percent of black children in Wallace's state attended segregated schools. By the fall of 1970, when doors reopened for the new term, that number dropped to eight percent. "The miracle has happened almost unnoticed in the South," Shultz told Nixon's cabinet that December.

Shultz, given the leadership by the president, began with the assumption that the South would eventually have to accept integrated systems. Instead of establishing an adversarial relationship between federal and local authorities, he worked through grassroots leaders, including influential blacks, offering them federal funds to help expedite the task. That achievement, especially when contrasted with his position on busing, effectively damaged his credibility over civil rights. Ironically, some big city systems were, at that very moment, battlegrounds over court-ordered busing. "That was a helluva good job for Shultz," remarked a grateful Nixon many years later.

Notably, especially in view of the competition from Wallace, Nixon instructed Haldeman to instruct the White House staff that he was a conservative. As the chief of staff recorded the president's request, he explained that "he does not believe in integration, will carry out the law, nothing more." He was also determined to avoid dropping in on the predominantly black Watts district of Los Angeles, the scene of a severe urban conflagration just a few years earlier, because the gesture "could alienate whites" without winning over any blacks.

Another product of that period, but one that was not invented by his presidency, was the concept of "affirmative action." Nixon, however, during the actual process of working to wean American workers from their Democratic voting habits, reinforced Johnson's Executive Order 11246 that required employers fulfilling contracts to do work for the federal government to make sure their hiring practices were not discriminatory.

The phrase became synonymous with positive steps to increase the representation of groups historically excluded from employment, especially minorities and women. Their newfound advantage was compensatory *preferential* selection. As early as March 27, 1969, Nixon reminded one of the country's leading business groups, the National Association of Manufacturers, that the failure rate for minority entrepreneurs was even greater than for small businessmen in general. On May 5, he followed through with an executive order that created an Office of Minority Business within the Department of Commerce, to be coordinated with the Small Business Administration.

Nixon then fought to maintain appropriations. He explained that the program was designed to have builders "set specific goals of minority manpower utilization" to complement existing federal provisions. Implicit in the entire action was the assumption that the construction industry's history of exclusion simply allowed no confidence in its own recruitment methods and self-reform actions. The program went into effect in September 1969, survived congressional opposition, and expanded to include about 55 plans in various cities by late 1972, when Executive Order 4 cast a wider net over American institutions and the process of minority hiring. Nevertheless, it continued to be known as the Philadelphia Plan, because that was where the first agreement was made.

At the outset, some conservatives failed to grasp what organized labor and pro-black groups saw right away, as Ehrlichman noted for the president, as an effort to drive "a wedge between the Democrats and labor which has stretched the membrane," while conceding that it could still become a "slow and reasonable" approach to civil rights if pursued "without undue zeal."

Nixon's response to Supreme Court vacancies and his opportunities for appointments were far less ambiguous. He moved quickly in 1969 when the Senate failed to confirm Johnson nominee Abe Fortas by replacing retired Chief Justice Earl Warren with Warren Burger, a Minnesota Eisenhower–Harold Stassen Republican who seemed reliably strong about applying a strict constructionist view of the Constitution.

Nixon's subsequent messages of how the Warren Court should be transformed were directed to civil rights resisters generally. He found a succession of nominees in the South, first Clement F. Haynsworth, Jr., of South Carolina, then G. Harrold Carswell of Florida. The latter was especially indefensible for his white supremacist background; both, however, were rejected. Finally, Nixon went for a Minnesota friend of Chief Justice Burger, Harry Blackmun, who was easily confirmed. Later, in 1971, following the resignations of justices Hugo Black, an outstanding liberal, and John M. Harlan, Nixon successfully rounded out the court with Lewis F. Powell, Jr., a Virginia conservative, and William Rehnquist, an Arizona Goldwaterite, who became chief justice after Burger's retirement. Nixon had reshaped the court to suite the tastes of the post-Democratic, anti-liberal thrust. By any definition, Nixon had eroded the Supreme Court liberalism that dated back to Roosevelt's time.

* * *

George Wallace continued to loom as a possibly decisive force. As vital as raising money was Nixon's need to get the civil rights dilemma out of the way before 1972, and Wallace excelled at making political hay out of the issue. Harry Dent, the Texas Republican state chairman, warned that "in 1970 and 1972 it is entirely possible that Wallace and the American Independent Party candidates will be a factor in many U.S. Senate and congressional races. I certainly hope the Nixon administration is fully aware of what the consequences of this might be. It has more than just 'southern' implications."

On July 19, 1970, the president wrote on his pad, "Need to handle Wallace." The governor's success was undermining Nixon's own gains in the South. The only feasible counterattack, to avoid losing out on those crucial electoral votes, would be by pursuing the Wallace strategy vigorously against the Democrats. Deprive them of their northern working-class support by hanging the "race-liberal-student tag" on them. "Put in question," he wrote on his pad.

"Demos stand for (?) principles. Do you support party which stands for those principles." Moreover, he was more convinced than ever that it was a mistake to assume that "RN. picked up [support] as he became more liberal on Race, Welfare, environment, troop withdrawal."

A strong Democratic candidate in 1972, such as Edmund Muskie, who had been so impressive when running alongside Humphrey, could compete with Nixon so effectively in the north that those southern electors would be absolutely essential. School desegregation as a live issue, however, could easily undermine Nixon's position there. With Nixon needing to keep an eye on the north as well, he would be at a real disadvantage if he tried to tackle the South's most defiant voice. It was not hard to believe that Wallace might achieve in 1972 the electoral deadlock he had failed to create in 1968, especially if he once again ran on a third party line.

Nixon's maneuvers were not designed to be racist but politically defensive. They were attempts to restrain Wallace's appeal by moderating what conservatives considered as the excesses of recent Democratic reforms. Nixon, supporter of the Court's *Brown* decision, took up the dissenting cause by opposing busing as a means of implementing desegregation. At the same time, in perhaps his most cynical maneuver, he had quietly engineered what amounted to the transformation of southern school patterns in compliance with the Court, with the bottom-line objective of depriving Wallace of his signature issue as he tried to regain Alabama's governorship against the incumbent, Albert B. Brewer, who had taken over from Wallace's proxy, his wife Lurleen, when she died of cancer in 1968.

Nixon made two moves, in 1970 and again in 1971, to cut off Wallace "at the pass," as he later put it. His campaign fund-raising machinery, the Committee to Re-Elect the President, helped to fund Albert Brewer's primary campaign to keep Wallace from regaining the governorship. Wallace nevertheless won, defeating Brewer, and strengthening himself as a potential third-party presidential candidate for 1972.

For Nixon, the challenge became greater. The Alabaman clearly had the potential to draw more votes from him than from the Democratic candidate. Here, once again, as had been done under the Roosevelt and Kennedy administrations, but to a far more sweeping extent, Nixon and his staff used the Internal Revenue System as an instrument of presidential leverage to reward friends and punish enemies. Conversations recorded on White House tapes confirm the almost casual use of such private records as a weapon against actual or potential candidates. Their names emerged during the subsequent Watergate hearings and the release of the tapes. Included were such individuals as Senators Hubert Humphrey, George McGovern, and Edmund Muskie, and Democratic National Chairman Larry O'Brien. None loomed so prominently a threat to Nixon's political future as another senator on the list, Edward Moore (Ted) Kennedy, the younger brother of the two assassinated Kennedys, John and Robert. The latest Kennedy with presidential aspirations, and the glamour of the family name, had represented Massachusetts since his election in 1962.

In the Wallace case, the opportunity for the Nixon people to act came when Haldeman learned that the IRS was investigating political corruption in Alabama. He leaked the agency's findings to a well-connected, muckraking political newspaper columnist, Jack Anderson. Although Wallace himself was not about to be named, his brother Gerald, described by Nixon as a "bagman" for George's donors, would appear among at least a dozen businessmen involved in milking state contracts for millions of dollars.

Some of the precise details of what happened are still questionable, but, whatever the actual process, and exactly who did what, the outcome is clear. In mid-May of 1971, after spending a long weekend in Key Biscayne, Nixon returned to Washington aboard Air Force One, then to his southern speaking engagements. When he flew by helicopter from Mobile to Birmingham, Wallace went along for the ride, presumably to do business. Reporters focused on what was evidently an easy, warm Wallace-Nixon relationship. Winton Blount, an Alabaman then serving as Nixon's postmaster general, remained in the state for further meetings with the governor. Wallace told him that he and the president were both primarily concerned with keeping a liberal Democrat out of the White House.

When the grand jury in Montgomery, Alabama's capital, met again that September, it returned indictments against some business and political leaders who had broken with Wallace between 1968 and 1971. The name of Gerald Wallace was conspicuously missing.

Governor Wallace, meanwhile, told his chief fundraiser, Tom Turnipseed, that he was thinking of becoming a Democrat again. Gerald, who had earlier been notably depressed, told Turnipseed after the Wallace-Nixon Air Force One trip that his tax troubles were over. The Justice Department later followed through by ending the investigation of Gerald Wallace and dismissing the grand jury. Alabama's governor then announced that he would make another run for the presidency, this time not as a third-party candidate, but as a contender in the Democratic primaries. Wallace's closest biographer, Dan Carter, who interviewed Turnipseed, has concluded that "Whether or not an explicit deal was made, Wallace's decision to abandon his third-party effort was an act of extraordinary importance for the Nixon re-election campaign strategists. No longer would they have to worry about responding to Wallace; he was the Democrats' problem."

8

Nixon and the World

In 1969, events continued to favor Nixon. White House optimists focused on the strong economic trends. The respected Gallup poll showed Nixon's approval ratings holding in the mid-sixties. The president also welcomed a burst of inspirational patriotism when *Apollo II*, with astronauts Neil A. Armstrong and Edwin "Buzz" Aldrin, Jr., landed at Tranquility Base on the moon. "Hello Neil and Buzz," said Nixon in a conversation that traveled through the universe, "I am talking to you by telephone from the Oval Room in the White House, and this certainly has to be the most historic telephone call ever made from the White House."

In upstate New York, a festival promoted as "Woodstock" brought together top stars—Jimi Hendrix, Janis Joplin, and Joan Baez—for a rock concert, the high point of the decade's newly chic counterculture. More than 300,000 strong, they camped out despite thunderstorms and mud, some stripping down in the August heat, at a 600-acre farm in the tiny Catskill town of Bethel, some 70 miles northwest of New York City—anti-Nixon and antiwar, they epitomized the underside of American culture gone wild.

That July, a "gift" came from the island of Chappaquiddick just off Martha's Vineyard along the southern coast of Massachusetts. Ted Kennedy, the sole survivor among

the four sons of Joseph P. Kennedy and the most prominent living member of the illustrious family, steered his
borrowed automobile off a precarious wooden bridge and
into a pond near the village of Edgartown. The submerged
car came to rest on its roof in the midnight darkness.

Not until daylight were local authorities alerted. The
passenger in his car was last seen leaving the annual staff
reunion with the senator, who was thought to be drop-
ping her off at her motel. She was Mary Jo Kopechne, one
of the political aides in Bobby Kennedy's "boiler room."
The senator's responsibility for her death remained vague.
"Woman Passenger Killed, Kennedy Escapes in Crash;
Senator Tells Police He Wandered About in Shock After
Car Ran Off Bridge Near Martha's Vineyard," ran a *New
York Times* headline.

Nixon, intrigued by the incident and wondering how the
media would be treating the episode if it had happened to
one of *his* own people, told Haldeman that he wanted to
make sure that Kennedy did not escape responsibility for
what he assumed was negligence resulting from drunken-
ness. Ehrlichman dispatched Caulfield to Martha's Vineyard to dig up whatever could be used to destroy Kennedy;
he told his aides at Camp David that he had "to be certain
he doesn't get away with it." He also told Haldeman that
he wanted a 24-hour surveillance to catch Ted in "the sack
with one of his babes." But neither the White House nor
the local police got Kennedy on anything stronger than
"leaving the scene of an accident," for which he pleaded
guilty and received a suspended sentence of two months
in jail. He had, however, destroyed what remained of any
higher political aspirations, just what Nixon wanted.

Alone with his thoughts on the Labor Day weekend,
Nixon reflected on the impotence of his office. It was sup-
posed to be the most powerful in the world. "Each day
[is] a chance," he wrote on his pad, "to do something
memorable for some one," and then he added the thought

about "the need to be good in order to do good." The presidency was as much personal as administrative. He had to be the one to set the example, to inspire and instill pride; public confidence would respond to displays of strength, compassion, and competence, and the image of a chief executive who had some "joy" in what he was doing. Those words kept being repeated on his pad: joy, serenity, inspirational. The leadership he contemplated was in his hands.

No issue asked more of leadership than the ongoing war. "If for one month everybody would 'shut up' about the war," he told the cabinet at Camp David in September 1969, "we would be a long way toward getting it over."

He refused to become the "first American President to lose." With three years and three months left in office, he had plenty of time to turn around "the Vietnam thing" as far as the world was concerned. In Paris, the on-again-off-again "peace talks" had died, stalemated between North Vietnamese insistence on the immediate withdrawal of American troops and Washington's loyalty to the Thieu regime in the South. If we lost the war in Vietnam or pulled an elegant bug-out, Nixon reasoned, the United States would "retreat from the world," and the "*first defeat in history would destroy the confidence of the American people in themselves.*" It would all be over by the 1970 elections; "*we are going to be able by then to 'see the light at the end of the tunnel.'*" "One [casualty] is too many," he told a group of senators; but "it's moving," and the critics "won't look good in '70." With some bravado, he added, "Polls and editorials don't affect us much."

He kept pressing his staff, almost obsessively, for confirmation that the Communists were encouraged by the demonstrations and by critics' attacks on the administration. He was sure that an irresponsible part of the press, a small and atypical but influential group, along with the television networks (now collectively more commonly called "the media"), was, in effect, giving aid and comfort to the enemy. Almost from the moment he entered office, the Nixon White House, at the president's direct desire, started the process of generating "some non obvious ltrs [sic] to editors," allegedly from ordinary Americans, to condemn "biased" coverage by the press.

On May 14, his radio address had made wide-ranging proposals for peace in the Far East, including a mutual withdrawal of *all* outside forces within one year and a cease-fire carried out under international supervision. Everything was negotiable, he said, but the United States would reserve the rights of the South Vietnamese to determine their own future. All sides would have to renounce force so the people of South Vietnam could "determine their own political future without outside interference." It was not very different, he added, from what the United States had tried to achieve in Paris. Secretary of State Rogers arranged for Nixon to meet with President Thieu in Guam in mid-July. At a Pacific press conference on July 25, he laid down the Nixon Doctrine, which became the guideline for Vietnamization. Major responsibility for holding back the enemy would revert to indigenous fighters, who would gradually replace the Americans.

Nixon, after his brief stay in Guam, flew from the mid-Pacific for a much broader inspection of the southeastern region, and, before leaving Saigon in late July, began to scale down American operations. "How this war is ended," he told troops of the First Infantry Division in Vietnam, "may well determine what happens to peace and freedom in all of Asia."

Antiwar groups understood that, however doubtful the enterprise, the war would go on until there was an "honorable" completion of American objectives. Nothing like an exit was in sight. After the Nixon-Thieu meeting, and the announcement of the planned first withdrawal of 25,000 troops, a nod toward Vietnamization, some suspected that the two leaders were only going through "all the traditional motions."

Also, that May, the press reported leaked information about the "secret" bombing of Cambodia, a neutral neighbor of Vietnam, effectively exposing what had been kept from the American public. Urged by the military chiefs and endorsed by Kissinger, and then signed-off by the president, B-52 bombing missions had struck at targets masked by Pentagon records as routine missions against South Vietnam. Interjecting North Vietnam supply lines, Kissinger held, required knocking out enemy supply lines going through the jungle in Cambodia. "Hanoi's unopposed conquest of Cambodia," Kissinger later wrote in his memoirs, "would have been the last straw for South Vietnam," reflecting the American military's fear of North Vietnamese encroachment against the anti-Communist regime then holding the nation's capital in Phnom Penh.

All in all, before and after the raids were revealed, some 540,000 tons of bombs were dropped, with the loss of hundreds of citizens. Nixon, determined to have a firm hand on every aspect of foreign policy, was infuriated by evidence of leaks to the press about the Cambodian strikes. With Kissinger's approval, wiretaps were placed on the telephones of key aides.

Surveillance was not new to the presidency, but Nixon took it to a new level. Within the first two years of the administration, monitoring included tapping the phones of seven members of the National Security Council staff, three within the White House itself, one line in the Defense Department, and four belonging to newspaper reporters. The demands of national security, Nixon and his people argued, excused all efforts, legal or illegal, to root out subversion, all reminiscent of the fear that helped to spark his original rise to political power; antiwar dissidents replaced the home-grown "commies" of the '40s and '50s as the domestic villains. Three members of the NSC staff promptly protested the violation of a neutral nation by resigning. Two hundred and fifty Foreign Service officers protested to Rogers. FBI Director J. Edgar Hoover, meanwhile, separated his agency from the project, holding that it was merely supplying technical assistance but, nevertheless, the situation made him nervous. Attorney General Mitchell recognized that the administration was playing "a dangerous game" that might become "explosive," but the tapping stayed in place.

A climate of mutual distrust permeated the nation, from the streets to the national capital, and within the White House itself. To have, at that point, taken the administration's word that it was seeking an "honorable end" to the war would have required the sort of detachment from realities, especially given the existing distrust of Nixon, his objectives, and *his* honor. Even those who granted that the president's intentions were good suggested that that might not be enough to bring Thieu and his government into line.

Conditions had so deteriorated that the Nixon White House became more and more concerned with generating and targeting its own pro-war press coverage. When, that October, the president read in his daily news summary that fear of confrontation with student activists had led the University of Pennsylvania to retire its American flags for their own safety, he noted in the margin, "My god!"

His people were with him; the president knew that. The FBI sent him an article that appeared in Hanoi telling all about the shock felt by ordinary Americans, their sense of a country out of control; the working classes, especially, were feeling cheated, and their rage was toward liberal intellectuals and liberal politicians, hippies, and militant blacks. Some 85 percent of the American people, according to the FBI report, were angered by the lack of resistance to black militants and college demonstrators.

In survey after survey, Nixon's level of approval held up, with the figures usually rising when the survey was confined to whites; the lowest wage-earners were his weakest supporters, the highest his strongest, but there was significant overlapping at the point where earnings and awareness coincided. Ordinary American workers were with him on national honor and "God and country" issues but suspected Republican policies toward labor. Anger toward blacks and college students was especially strong; their demands threatened the patriotic, hardworking citizens' rightful place in the affluent society. Dissidents of all kinds, however, were not bothered that "middle Americans" were seeing themselves as the "ultimate victims." There was a "new majority" growing in the country, Nixon pointed out to an aide; "they live in rings around the cities, they're a new middle class." They constituted, as one journalist explained, an emerging blue-collar conservative vote that cared about the flag, about patriotism, about the work ethic.

For other Americans, principally the antiwar people, keeping Nixon in the White House meant escalation on the streets to counter events on the battlefield. Anything less than an impressive show of strength was no longer enough; the whole country had to take notice—newspapers, television—all the modern media. That reality moved the organizers of two big demonstrations planned for October, and an even larger turnout for the nation's capital one month later. Whatever the instinct to denounce the dissidents as hippies and kooks, the significant representation by the middle class could not be overlooked.

Even before the November demonstration, the White House tuned up its public relations campaign. Nixon fired off memo after memo to Haldeman and other aides urging a crackdown on the media's influence on public sympathy, just in case the excesses of the extremists had not already turned them off. Newspapers and television

Peace Demonstration
on the Mall,
November 15, 1969
© Bettmann/Corbis

stations received scores of letters, often under fictitious
White House–generated names, trying to set the record
straight about "unfair treatment."

Spiro Agnew became a potent weapon. He did not have
to be told when to "take off his gloves," and, with the aid
of speechwriter William Safire, he went to work blasting
the antiwar movement. The impact was dramatic, elevat-
ing him from an unknown—a "Spiro Who?"—to a household name, promoting a new upsurge of patriotism,
adorned with bumper stickers, American flag decals, and
lapel stick-pins.

On October 30, the vice president let loose in Harrisburg, Pennsylvania, by suggesting the possibility of "official

repression" of antiwar protesters. He described the demonstrators as "ideological eunuchs." He also declared that "If, in challenging, we polarize the American people, I say it is time for a positive polarization." An amused Nixon suggested that assassins now had a dilemma. "If they kill Nixon, they get Agnew." George Wallace, less impressed, doubted that Agnew's attacks would have "any real effect" unless they were "accompanied by policies as tough as the words."

The next test was the November 15 "march" on Washington. Meanwhile, Nixon himself was on an escalator that later led to a memorandum that directed Haldeman to develop a "list of those who are and will continue to be our major opponents between now and 1972. I refer not simply to press and TV, but the University community, religious organizations, finance; Eastern Establishment, the major Senate/House/Gubernatorial/Party leaders and minorities. . . . The purpose of this is to know who our opponents are and do nothing to build them up and to see that an intelligent program is developed to take them on where it is in our interest to do so."

Nixon skillfully achieved his objectives: undermining the counterculture, the entire antiwar movement, and the press, scornfully incorporating them into an alliance of enemies to create Agnew's memorable "positive polarization." And the president ran with it, leading a constituency he knew he could fire up.

He did so superbly, delivering his most effective presidential speech on November 3, appealing for the support of what he called "the silent majority." His televised message, termed by at least one liberal critic "a political masterpiece," was aimed to go over the heads of the media at a nation eager to believe in the righteousness of the cause. There would be no precipitate withdrawal, he vowed, and asked for perseverance until a "just peace through a negotiated settlement" became possible. "I know it may not be fashionable to speak of patriotism or national destiny these days," he said as he began his wind-down. "But I feel it is appropriate to do so on this occasion. . . . And so tonight—to you, the great silent majority of my fellow Americans—I ask for your support. . . . Let us understand: North Vietnam cannot defeat or humiliate the United States. Only Americans can do that." Even though Nixon later expressed doubts that "silent majority" was the most appropriate term, in practice he exploited the phrase to the hilt.

One week before going on the air, he advised Haldeman of the need to set up an "especially effective group" for the purpose "of monitoring the three television networks and hitting them hard on the positive side of the speech and taking them on if they take a negative view. I want this handled in more than a routine fashion and a strike force is to be set up for each network." He wanted another to track the *New York Times*, the *Washington Post*, and two major news magazines, "strongly supporting and taking them on for whatever critical comment they may indulge in." A follow-up might include organizing 300 or so letters from congressmen and senators backing the speech. Television was functioning as had powerful elements of the press in earlier days, spelling out to the public the political motives behind the president's speech, confirming his old image as a crafty politician instead of a statesman.

Two weeks after Agnew's Harrisburg speech, the National Mobilization Committee to End the War in Vietnam swamped Washington with at least a quarter of a million protesters, the largest antiwar demonstration in American history. They paraded down Pennsylvania Avenue, chanted peace slogans, and carried signs; then, in the frost of a harsh November day, they gathered at the foot of the Washington Monument.

On November 20, Agnew went to Montgomery, Alabama, and fired his next round, this time at the "irresponsible" press. His speech was powerful, effective, and targeted right at the *Washington Post*, the *New York Times*, and *Newsweek*. He did not mind, he said, that he had been called the "greatest polarizer" in American politics. But in fact it was those who marched up Pennsylvania and Constitution avenues who "sought to polarize the American people against the President's policy in Vietnam."

The political atmosphere suddenly filled with such "Agnewisms" as "radiclibs," who, he said when campaigning in Illinois, had taken over the Democratic Party. Then there were the "nattering nabobs of negativism," the "hopeless, hysterical hypochondriacs of history," and the charge that a "paralyzing permissive philosophy pervades every policy they espouse." No modern Republican president had ever made such a strong pitch for the backing of traditionally patriotic working-class Americans, once again fishing in Wallace waters.

Not clearly understood at the time, but more effective than anyone could have imagined, it suggested the creation of what Nixon came to call his "new majority." Agnew also kicked off what became better known for the rest of the century and thereafter as the "culture wars."

* * *

The private face of the administration's foreign policy apparatus, however, was a very different matter. "Nothing has a higher priority than bringing the war to a close," the president had told a group of cabinet wives five months before his silent majority speech, and then added, reassuringly, "we will make significant progress . . . in the next months."

Politics and strategic internationalism aside, Nixon would gladly have walked away from the war, or at least moved closer to the more conciliatory views of both

Rogers and Defense Secretary Melvin Laird. Reading an insightful news report that Washington "has been running a transparently thin bluff" by acting tough while really wanting "out," Nixon observed to Kissinger that it was "the heart of the matter." Most assuredly, the adviser for national security affairs digested that comment carefully as he instinctively monitored the president's mood. Seeing foreign policy as their mutual province, Kissinger tended to view Rogers "as an insensitive neophyte who threatened the careful design of our foreign policy."

For the most pragmatic military and strategic reasons, the Communists in Hanoi were reluctant to settle. The Ho Chi Minh regime pulled the strings of the National Liberation Front, which, in turn, worked with the Vietcong to undermine the government of South Vietnam. Half a million American troops were tied down; guerrilla fighters had eliminated just about any remaining sanctuaries around Saigon. Their success had notably helped to stigmatize the U.S. involvement and frustrate Johnson into ever deeper desperation about a war he could not win and dared not lose. Nixon was about to become the next victim.

More and more, it seemed, despite his tough, uncompromising stance, he was on the defensive, illustrated most vividly by the lack of an American president's freedom to comfortably visit campuses for even routine addresses. Nearly 3,000 bombings and more than 50,000 threats of planted bombs had taken place since the start of 1970.

As long as the war continued, divisions grew more serious at home, far from the Nixon promise of unity. Johnson had considered Vietnam something to get over with so he could get on with his Great Society. Nixon and Kissinger, as much as they weighed the political implications of continuing the fight, linked the war to the nation's long-range international interests.

When it came time to prop up his political supports, Nixon abandoned his solitude. He returned from a state visit to Europe that fall fearing that Republican prospects were bleak and that at least two Senate seats could be lost in that off-year election, with unemployment also showing an untimely rise. A brighter spot, unfortunately just as untimely in the opposite direction, was the all-too-recent-to-be-noticed emergence of inflation.

The cost of living had more than doubled since Nixon's inauguration, finally leveling off after an economic downturn earlier in the year. Ever since becoming president, Nixon had monitored the relative political damage of price gains vis-à-vis unemployment. He was more willing to risk inflation than unemployment, a point he made clear to Arthur Burns, his replacement for William McChesney Martin, not a Nixon favorite, as head of the Federal Reserve Bank.

* * *

His biggest gamble was yet to come. His good friend Bebe reminded him that "This is the big play," words that the president recorded on a canary legal pad. Yes, he thought to himself, as he sat alone pen in hand, he needed to make the "big decision," and "get it right." This was no time to worry about his "fluctuation in popularity polls[.]" He thought about little else over that weekend.

On Tuesday, before a gathering of military and patriotic groups, he revealed that he would soon make an announcement about how he planned to tackle the buildup of enemy forces along the Cambodian border. Charles Colson took notes and observed the "somber and very serious tone to the meeting." The president, he added, "was obviously very preoccupied and concerned with the Cambodian situation and he imparted the same degree of seriousness to the group."

The night before the speech, scheduled for a nationally televised address on Thursday, November 30, was a restless one for Nixon. Unable to sleep until at least 1:00 A.M., he got up for good at about 5:30 and went to the Executive Office Building (EOB) at about 8:00 A.M. He kept revising the language, and Rosemary Woods, his secretary, kept typing. During time-outs, he called Haldeman about locating his new pool table in the EOB because he decided it wouldn't fit in the solarium, which awed his chief of staff, who thought that it was "Absolutely astonishing he could get into trivia on [sic] brink of biggest step he's taken so far. Haldeman, meanwhile, took the precaution of discussing with Ehrlichman the wisdom of sending troops to New Haven as a standby force to head off possible violence during protests at Yale. "Will be a tough couple of days," he noted.

"The time has come for action," he told the nation on Thursday night. Cambodia was a neutral nation, he explained, but its territory was violated by the creation of enemy sanctuaries on its soil. Our mission was to clean out "major North Vietnamese and Vietcong-occupied territories" and wipe out "the headquarters for the entire Communist military operation in South Vietnam, COSVN [Central Office of South Vietnam]. He declared that he would rather be a one-term president than the first to lose a war. "If when the chips are down," he said near the end of his brief but dramatic message, "the world's most powerful nation acts like a pitiful helpless giant, the forces of totalitarianism and anarchy will threaten free nations and free institutions throughout the world," a restatement of the belief that Communist success in Southeast Asia would inevitably result in "free" adjacent states falling like dominoes. As Nixon told his staff afterward, "We are doing this to buy the time we need for Vietnamization." The destruction of their potential to attack was more important than how many were actually killed. "It takes ten months to build up this complex, and we're tearing the living bejeesus out of it. Anything that walked is gone after that barrage, and the B-52 raids."

Nixon probably did achieve one objective, buying additional time for Vietnamization and setting back the offensive capabilities of North Vietnam, at least temporarily. The COSVN headquarters, however, was far from a "Pentagon East." It sat in a corner of the Cambodian jungle that jutted into South Vietnam, an elusive mobile headquarters consisting of a series of huts originally thought to be located within South Vietnam itself.

The announcement of the "incursion" kicked up more hell than even he had expected. Tens of thousands of protesters, with estimates going as high as 100,000, descended on Washington, and buses were lined up to encircle the White House as a protective barrier. The man who allegedly had a secret plan for ending the war had instead widened it. The radicalization of dissent seemed complete.

Just a few days later, after a night of rioting and fires at the campus of Kent State University in Ohio, four young protesters were killed by National Guardsmen, who had been sent by Governor James Rhodes to restore order. Hundreds of miles away, at Jackson State College in Mississippi, police fired indiscriminately into the dormitory of black women students, killing two and wounding nine. "I think we have to recognize that there is a great deal of fear among adults today and that the feeling of opposition to the war and the Cambodian strike runs deeper on the campus than has anything in recent years," advised a memo to the president from his director of communications. "The daily news reports conveyed a sense of turmoil bordering on insurrection," Nixon later wrote in his memoirs.

He went to the Pentagon the next day and gave a little talk about the student dissenters. His words, as recorded in the official papers of his presidency, were as follows:

> You think of those kids out there. I say 'kids.' I have seen them. They are the greatest.
> You see these bums, you know, blowing up the campuses. Listen, the boys that are on the college campuses today

are the luckiest people in the world, going to the greatest universities, and here they are burning up the books, I mean
storming around about this issue—I mean you name it—get
rid of the war; there will be another one.

Violence even reached the heart of the capitalist establishment, New York City's Wall Street financial center. On Fri-
day, May 8, student antiwar demonstrators, attempting to
attract lunch-hour street traffic, were suddenly assaulted by
a band of construction workers. Wearing hard hats, which
had become the badge of their trade and symbol of counter-
dissent, they chased the youngsters through the mob of
amazed spectators, battering heads whenever they could
and scattering the victims throughout the downtown
canyons, wounding about 70 before it was all over.

The police watched with mixed feelings of horror and
delight as the hard hats then took off toward city hall.
Meanwhile, another angry mob, provoked by missile-
throwing students, invaded Pace University, smashing win-
dows with crowbars and clubs and lashing out at those
who blocked their way. Other workers ripped off a Red
Cross banner at the gate of Trinity Church because they
mistook it for a Vietcong flag.

Moreover, as a military maneuver, the value of the
Cambodian invasion was questionable. Nixon later claimed
that it "had demonstrated Vietnamization was working"
and that it spurred the process of pacification. Even disre-
garding the domestic political cost of the operation, the
price also included new restraints limiting future exten-
sions of the war into Cambodia or Laos, which had been
carried out before Nixon came to power. The domestic and
military liabilities indeed combined to hasten demands for
troop withdrawals and, ironically, to further delay Nixon's
ability to achieve what he called "peace with honor."

At the same time, it helped to create a Cambodian
tragedy. Destabilized internally, Lon Nol's rule ultimately

led to the country's takeover by the Communist Khmer Rouge headed by Pol Pot, one of history's chief mass murderers. The Cambodian genocide that followed claimed some 1.7 million lives, with millions more forcibly relocated or sent into forced labor. Ethnic Vietnamese and Chinese Cambodians were decimated, and, within four years, 15 percent of the rural Khmers and 25 percent of urban residents perished.

* * *

Nixon's postmortem account of such days of agitation conveyed a detachment that can variously be described as offering brave, strong, determined leadership; or, to critics, a presidential response that was indifferent and insensitive to the rebellions tearing the nation he had vowed to reunite.

He had not held a televised news conference for more than three months. His discomfort was obvious. As he faced the newsmen on May 8, only hours after the Wall Street head-bashing, there was little of the administration's familiar combative style, no hint of anything resembling Vice President Spiro Agnew's verbal assaults. He was earnest, almost eager to please his critics. He understood their dismay. He shared their objectives. He, too, wanted to shorten the war.

His responses to questions from the newsmen were not adversarial. He supplied just the sort of information they wanted. The Cambodian invasion had gone better than expected, and he promised that 150,000 additional American troops would be withdrawn from South Vietnam by the spring. In response to whether he really intended to move from an era of confrontation with the Soviet Union to an era of negotiation, he predicted a significant agreement. "The Soviet Union," he explained, "has just as great an interest as we have in seeing that there is some limitation on nuclear arms." Then, in an obvious bid to identify with the concerns of youth, he recalled his own early days in Congress when, in opposition to President Truman, he, like the students, had "the luxury of criticism because they can criticize and if it doesn't work out then they can gloat over it, or if it does work out, the criticism will be forgotten." He had been there himself, and he knew how it felt.

Satisfied with his performance, the president returned to the executive mansion. "I was agitated and uneasy as the events of the last few weeks raced through my mind," he wrote, also recalling that he "slept for a few hours," but the telephone log lists 50 separate calls that were made after the press conference. They began at 9:22 P.M. and concluded with a call to his valet, Manolo Sanchez, at 4:22 A.M., leaving hardly enough time for much more than a catnap. William Safire, a Nixon speechwriter, concludes that he must have slept sometime between his 1:55 A.M. and 3:38 A.M. calls.

A little after 4:00 A.M., the president walked into the Lincoln Sitting Room. He put a Philadelphia Orchestra recording of Rachmaninoff's First Piano Concerto on the turntable. Sanchez heard the music and came in to ask if he needed any help. He found the president looking through the window toward the students who were beginning to gather on the Ellipse. Beyond that grassy area was the Washington Monument, at the southern edge of the planned demonstration.

Safire later noted that it was the "most impulsive, and perhaps most revealing night of Nixon's Presidency. . . . He broke out of the cocoon that separates the President from the rest of humanity for three hours, enjoyed a taste of real life and the bitter aftertaste." His impulse seemed understandable, but Nixon was communing as much with inspiration as with reality.

Bud Krogh, the aide who discovered that the president had wandered out that night, found him just inside the Lincoln Memorial, at the foot of the Great Emancipator's statue.

The communion clearly inspired awe in him. It bolstered his need to reach out to be understood, to plead the cause from the perspective of the president, the leader, the man with the responsibility for making decisions that cannot be fully understood by those who may have to pay the price. He told the surprised little group of students that gathered around him about his own youth. "Do you realize that many of us, when we were your age, were also willing to die for what we believed in, and are willing to do so today?" "I know that probably most of you think I'm an SOB, but I want you to know that I understand just how you feel." He was reminded of his own days as a law student at Duke. He recalled that his desire for peace had led him to believe in Chamberlain and to oppose Churchill. He had to. He was raised in a Quaker family. "I was as close to being a pacifist as anybody could be in those times," he said. Then he added that the great question of war and peace was really in their hands, as Lincoln had told his countrymen in his first inaugural address. Nixon then urged his listeners to travel, to get to know the complex world. "I told them," he wrote soon afterward, "my great hopes that during my administration, and certainly during their lifetime, that the great mainland of China would be opened up so that we could know the 700 million people who live in China who are one of the most remarkable people on earth." To the young people nearby, he said, "Try to understand what we are doing. Sure you came here to demonstrate and shout your slogans on the Ellipse. That is all right. Just keep it peaceful. . . . Remember, I feel just as deeply as you do about this." He started to explain details about the progress of the strategic arms limitations talks until he saw their attention beginning to wander.

Their hatred for war was understandable, he said. Their feelings were commendable. He urged them not to go from that reaction to a condemnation of our whole system and everything it stood for. Constructive achievements were possible. For example, he explained, most of them came from campuses where racial desegregation had been carried out. But that only created a new kind of segregation. While blacks and whites were now attending classes together, they seemed to have even less contact with each other than before. "You must find a way to communicate with the blacks in your universities," Krogh heard him say.

Nixon walked down to the base of the memorial. At that point, he saw a group of girls in their early twenties. Krogh asked one of them if she had had any sleep. She confirmed that their night had been spent driving to Washington for the demonstration; they had just arrived and had no idea of where they could sleep. Nixon, eager to greet the later arrivals, asked one girl her age. She said she was twenty-four. "That's Tricia's age," he replied, which seemed to be appropriate small talk. Another young woman, also answering a presidential question, said she was from Syracuse University. The association with the school and its athletic program seemed obvious to Nixon. In an effort to continue the conversation, he noted the prominence of her school's football team.

That parting comment, made just before Nixon and his party left the memorial at 5:55 A.M. somehow reduced the sunrise visit in his critics' eyes to a trivial, bumbling, insensitive effort to "use" the kids. Only a few days after he had called violent students "bums," Safire wrote, he "had compounded his error by talking condescendingly about trivial matters like football or visiting foreign cities with students who had come in seriousness to protest about the war." Indeed, the young woman from Syracuse who had talked to the president told a reporter, "Here we come from a university that's completely uptight, on strike, and when we told him where we were from, he talked about the football team. And when someone said he was from California, he talked about surfing."

The incident, declared the *Washington Post*, was "a dialogue of the deaf." The effort was dismissed as another example of presidential callousness. As White House Chief of Staff Haldeman then wrote in a memorandum to speechwriter Ray Price, the treatment of the encounter made Nixon realize "that it would have made more news from the standpoint of the students for him to engage in a spiritual dialogue with them about why we were in Cambodia—why we haven't ended the war sooner—the morality of the war, etc. . . . but as he evaluated the situation . . . [he] felt that perhaps the major contribution he could make to them was 'to try to lift them a bit out of the miserable intellectual wasteland in which they now wander aimlessly around.'"

Barely one month later, a White House siege mentality clearly on the mind of a president rapidly losing whatever distinctions existed between the interests of the presidency and the needs of the country, he met with his intelligence chiefs. There they were in the Oval Office, the president and his national security apparatus, individuals composing the National Security Agency, the Defense Intelligence Agency, as well as J. Edgar Hoover of the FBI and Richard Helms of the CIA. They heard a sweeping proposal presented by an ambitious fourth-level member of the staff, Tom Huston. It addressed itself to the "new and grave crisis in our country," in which countless numbers of Americans were "determined to destroy our society." Huston's specifics, forwarded to the White House less than three weeks later, contained familiar World War II–era internal security measures. Huston advised that some of what he noted were "illegal" procedures, provided "also the most fruitful tools and can produce the kind of intelligence which cannot be obtained in any other fashion. . . ." Moreover, advised the young man, the use of "surreptitious entry" by government agents would clearly be illegal."

Nixon, after expressing his own reservations to Haldeman, nevertheless passed on the Huston recommendations, but the final veto was left to Hoover. Determined to keep full control of the FBI's information, the director hesitated about signing off on any illegal procedures without direct presidential authorization. Attorney General Mitchell agreed. Nixon then withdrew Huston's schemes. The final decision, Haldeman noted, was as affected by the nature of the messenger as by the message. But Nixon then told his chief of staff about the youthful dissenters, we "have to find out who controls them" and need to get "our guys to rough them up at demonstrations."

* * *

Unfortunately, Nixon discovered, even the flattening of inflation numbers that fall had little impact as he undertook his ambitious cross-country speechmaking. Popular opinion, still largely ignoring the connection between the commitment in Southeast Asia and economics, was more agitated by the antiwar crowd than by the price of bread. News about the invasion of Cambodia and the subsequent protests, especially the Kent State killings, cut short a market rally. The Dow-Jones index fell 17 points the day after the Kent State incident, carrying the average all the way down to 621, but "the feared earthquake" never came and the market returned to 700 by the end of May. But the economy was then hurt by a six-week strike of General Motors, forcing unemployment to hit 7.5 percent of blue-collar workers by the fourth quarter of the year, and dooming Republican hopes for major gains among a vital segment of the Silent Majority. In October, Nixon told Ehrlichman, "Every statistic this month is bad."

The president responded by outdoing any previous incumbent in campaigning across the country, covering 17,241 miles in 23 days and visiting 22 states. His trip included a carefully staged encounter at San Jose on October 29. Demonstrators were encouraged to stand right behind the barricades near his car. As though on cue, they responded by pelting the vehicle with eggs and rocks as the president flashed his "V" salute and said, "That's what they hate to see," a scene that gave him dramatic television material for an election eve appeal to Middle America. Finally, with voters due to go to the polls on November 3, he returned to vote from his Western White House at San Clemente on California's Pacific shore.

It truly was the year of the "non-emerging Republican majority." Democratic candidates did better than in 1968 by an average of three percent, improving from 1.1 million two years earlier to a total of 4.5 million in 1970, a margin inflated, reported the Gallup pollsters, by ex-Wallace voters, who went Democratic by more than two to one. Even in the South, there were more losses than gains. With Wallace preparing for 1972, the Times suggested that Nixon might have to reconsider his strategy. Democrats had their biggest victory by taking away eleven governorships, always an important factor for an upcoming presidential election. The congressional picture appeared less gloomy. The Republicans gained two Senate seats while losing a dozen in the House. Such congressional shifts were relatively minor, hardly what one might expect given the situation. Reacting from San Clemente the next day, Nixon quickly disputed reports that he was disappointed at the outcome.

On the contrary, he said, there were reasons for optimism. Polls confirmed Nixon's hope that the protestors themselves would become more controversial than the war itself, a process that the administration had fanned when the president himself announced during the campaign that 40,000 more troops would be withdrawn before Christmas. Merely part of the 150,000 already announced at the start of the year, it nevertheless provided a clear signal when combined with Defense Secretary Laird's prediction that the draft would end by the summer of 1973.

But even as Nixon analyzed what had happened, and as optimistic as he appeared in public about the results, he could not shake the general consensus that the administration had not succeeded, that the politics of polarization had actually backfired against Republican candidates. Even if surveys showed public approval holding above 60 percent, he could not escape the sense that he and Agnew were offering negative leadership, just as he realized that he had to take the full plunge into domestic politics. He no longer wanted to meet with those groups, he told Ehrlichman shortly after the election, "where we have nothing to gain at all. . . . We will continue to get 8 to 10% of the Jewish vote and there is nothing that I can do that will get more."

One particular image about that 1970 election became unforgettable. The veteran of the Checkers speech and televised debates with John F. Kennedy chafed at the contrasting scenes of Ed Muskie, looking eminently presidential and in a full color on the tube while delivering a campaign talk from his rustic house in Maine, while perfectly awful black and white pictures showed the president—looking more like a flunky running for district attorney, John Mitchell noted—shouting harshly amid the tumultuous crowd of protesters at San Jose, California, demeaning to himself and to his office. The jarring reminder about the importance of images, Nixon noted in a memo to Haldeman, emphasized that, "in this age of television, technical quality is probably more important than the content of what is said."

9

Alone in the Lincoln Sitting Room

On December 6, Nixon worked alone in the Lincoln Sitting Room organizing his thoughts. He compiled a long list of dos and don'ts for press conferences; TV specials; radio messages; telephone calls; letters; meetings with his staff, cabinet, and congressional leaders; discussion groups; maybe even some surprise speaking stops. "Fill the Canvass," he wrote; "lead 'up to the hilt.' Every day is the last. Make it count . . . . Everybody must feel he is participating & contributing."

They were indeed troubling, those early days in 1971. Not since the 1958 recession was there as much concern over the health of the economy, wages and prices—almost as worrisome as the war itself. The inflation that Nixon had thought under control before the election was quite obvious. A Gallup survey underscored the melancholy news by reporting that "the Nixon administration is facing the same crisis in public confidence regarding the Vietnam War that confronted President Johnson's administration." Then came the real dig: "This is apparent both with respect to a 'credibility gap' and the President's handling of the war." Even his prized reputation for strength showed slippage, but, still, only 22 percent thought he was "weak."

In March, the president spoke out on a war matter he had preferred to downplay: the holding of Americans as prisoners-of-war (POWs) by the Communists in Southeast Asia. Stirring up the issue, as had many Democrats, he feared would only harden North Vietnamese negotiating points at peace talks. Public anxiety was understandable. H. Ross Perot, the Texas businessman who overflowed with money, had already turned worries about the servicemen into what one key Nixon aide, Colson, has described as "one of the most effective con jobs I ever saw in the White House" by promising $30 million to support a POW public relations campaign." All Perot really achieved, aside from a trip to Paris with wives and children of the imprisoned bearing Christmas presents for the POWs, was personal access to the president for his own purposes. Nixon tried to reason with the public by asking for their "continued dedication and continued public understanding, for the sake of the prisoners, for the sake of their families, and for the sake of human decency."

* * *

On March 29, an Army court-martial found a twenty-six-year-old platoon commander, First Lieutenant William Calley, Jr., guilty of the murder of 22 South Vietnamese civilians at My Lai in 1968. (The estimated number of fatalities varied all the way from 109 to 567.) Two days later, Calley was sentenced to life imprisonment.

First revealed by investigative reporter Seymour Hersh, the murders at the village quickly called "Pinkville" by the U.S. military were played as a victory over a bunch of "Reds." The incident, which gave no hint of the full extent of atrocities during the war, "could prove costly to the United States," warned Defense Secretary Laird. "Domestically," he also told Nixon, "it will provide grist for the mills of antiwar activists."

As Haldeman has pointed out, the Calley affair "became a political football for the left and for the media." The conviction clearly outraged the public. Calley had surely been scapegoated by the Army, and the White House was overwhelmed by protests. "The general public reaction has been stupendous, and we can't simply ignore it," Haldeman noted in his diary. George Wallace, one of Calley's first visitors, told the press that the conviction meant that "Every time a soldier seeks out the enemy, he will be tried for murder." Nixon's sympathy was clear. He ordered the convicted officer released from the stockade at Fort Benning and confined to his base while the conviction was being reviewed. His internal polls, which had indicated a 96 percent awareness of the verdict, also showed that the president's approval rating had zoomed upward by 13 points. Calley's prison term was later scaled down. After a U.S. district court in Georgia overturned his conviction, President Gerald Ford later ordered his release.

* * *

Early in 1971, Democrats, following through from the congressional elections with a fair degree of confidence, made some loud noises about keeping Nixon from a second term. Senator George McGovern, the "prairie populist" from South Dakota, supporter of the leftist-backed Henry Wallace in 1948 and now actively against the war, quit his chairmanship of the Democratic Reform Mission. The mission was designed to prepare for the party's next convention in a way that would "open up the political process and encourage the widest possible citizen participation in party matters at all levels." McGovern then announced his own presidential candidacy. Nixon's other competition seemed less way-out. A national trial-heat of the race for the White House published in February showed Muskie actually ahead of Nixon by three points, drawing 43 percent. Wallace, fulfilling his part of the bargain by running as a Democrat, was attracting 11 percent.

The next few weeks brought a different atmosphere around the White House, one very evident to the press corps. There was a "new mood there," noted a *Times* writer, "which presumably reflects the president's own. His oratory has become more conciliatory, his approaches to the press and the Congress more open." He even granted an interview to four correspondents. He told them that he would now "wear my hat as President of the United States."

He was weighing his next steps. Ten days after meeting with the reporters, he finally acted on an old source of irritation, Howard Hughes. Practically everybody who was anybody was on the "take" from Hughes, including Lawrence O'Brien, the chairman of the Democratic National Committee. Party chairmanships were then very much on the president's mind. He had just chosen Senator Robert Dole of Kansas to head the Republicans. But now, to expose the hypocrisy of the other side, he sent a memo to Haldeman. "It would seem that the time is approaching," he wrote, "when Larry O'Brien is held accountable for his retainer with Hughes. Bebe has some information on this although it is, of course, not solid but there is no question that one of Hughes' people did have O'Brien on a very heavy retainer for 'services rendered' in the past. Perhaps Colson should make a check."

Howard Hughes, the eccentric and well-known billionaire, was the most powerful and fattest cat of them all. A biographer has estimated that his contracts from the public purse came to an average of $1.7 million every day. Nixon, of course, by definition, was hardly unique among Hughes's connections. But he was the most durable, and the connection assumed the character of a mutual intrigue.

His worth, estimated at more than $1.5 billion, then made him just about the richest man in America; even if not literally true, it hardly mattered. If he was not Croesus, he was a splendid stand-in. Exuding that much money attracted all the eligible power brokers; he could, with that kind of clout and reputation, destroy as easily as build. His obsession with germs became the chief explanation for the hypochondria that had led to his self-imposed isolation in the years before his death.

But the most impressive flow of cash came after he had been forced out of the movie business "in the form of a check" for $546 million that closed his sale of Trans-World Airlines. His hobbies ultimately became big corporations. By the time Nixon entered the White House, Hughes had taken over a large chunk of Las Vegas and had clearly established economic dominance over Nevada. In 1974, the government resisted an indictment that accused him of conspiring with three associates of Hughes Air West, Inc. His lucrative defense trade made Hughes the single largest private contractor for the CIA.

A review of his connections questions the considerable degree of involvement with Nixon; and if not with him personally, with enough associates to establish a strong pattern: Donald and Hannah Nixon, and, most prominently, Bebe Rebozo. The Hughes connection was often uncomfortable and awkward for Nixon, which made his later acceptance of additional Hughes money through Rebozo even more inexplicable.

Nixon remained forever haunted by the Hughes connection. Little was more self-evident to the president than that those ties had hurt him in the past. And, having been assured that O'Brien had a similar relationship with the billionaire, evidence that he had remained on Hughes's payroll while Democratic chairman would be a devastating ten-score strike against the opposition. The Hughes-O'Brien relationship intrigued the president, a counterbalance of his own involvement, and possibly meaty for its potential political value.

A chronology of Hughes's loans, together with IRS actions, compiled by the Nixon White House during the next year, was finally turned over to Ehrlichman by Dean, who also collected suggested names for a White House "enemies" list.

Then, having in one way or another dealt with the chairmen of both parties, Nixon worked on his vows of nonpartisanship. With a small group of friends, he set up what would become, in effect, his own campaign operation, led mainly by Maurice Stans and his personal attorney, Herbert Kalmbach; others were readily available. His interests would be protected. He explained that "I want to be in the position where I can honestly say the White House does not have its hand in the political maneuvering that is going to begin the moment the new Congress comes in session."

The whole thing was perfectly in line with keeping the party itself distant from the Nixon operation, including the nomination process, the election and inauguration, and the subsequent scandals that fell under the collective name Watergate. Hugh Sloan, the treasurer, accumulated more than $1 million in his Washington office safe alone, but more cash was placed in deposit boxes in New York, Los Angeles, and Miami. Some was laid out in advance, along with many other purposes, for those recruits to spy on Democratic campaigns and report back. The sources of the funds included several executives and companies that were in trouble with the Justice Department or Internal Revenue Service. More money came from sources seeking government contracts; they arrived in various forms, wire transfers, corporate checks, personal checks, third-party checks, and cash. Speechwriter Safire named the operation the Citizens Committee for the Re-election of the President, assuming it would go under the acronym of CRP, failing to anticipate the vulnerability of how the term itself, "CREEP," could be mocked by the media and the administration's critics. In February 1971, when the committee opened for business on Pennsylvania Avenue, polls showed Muskie with a three-point lead.

* * *

An especially threatening May Day demonstration around the White House heightened dangers. Tens of thousands of antiwar people were in the city, disrupting all normal functions and services. They had to be countered by the District's police force just to minimize the damage, which was largely the result of pell-mell rampaging. The White House itself seemed besieged, and the sound of cherry bombs was audible from inside; the normal usual security detachment was reinforced. All around the White House, just as during the massive outpouring one year earlier, a wall of buses provided additional protection. In Georgetown, near the university, troops lined M Street and Wisconsin Avenue. Police ordered protesters out of Potomac Park and arrested those who resisted, herding them by the hundreds to RFK Stadium, which was then likened to a "concentration camp." Ehrlichman, concerned about what was happening at the stadium, kept in touch with Attorney General Mitchell, who seemed unable to explain why so many were being arbitrarily confined. Ehrlichman's notes for that Sunday evening indicate that the arrest number had reached 6,000.

At about 8:00 P.M., the domestic affairs adviser saw the president. Nixon was fuming. Frustrated, he wanted to lash back, but his political instincts were intact. He envisioned an outraged nation seeing pictures of their national capital being stormed by countless numbers of wild militants. Angrily, anticipating the political impact of the images relayed by the media, he turned to Ehrlichman and said, "Be sure police are hurt tomorrow. . . . Be sure McGovern can't avoid [the responsibility for] these demonstrations."

From all this, it followed quite naturally to Nixon that he go to "war" against the continued publication by the *New York Times* of the Pentagon's still-classified internal history of the war. The Pentagon Papers, as they came to be known, constituted a documented history of the American involvement in Vietnam from its start through the Johnson years. Daniel Ellsberg, a Defense Department consultant who helped write the still classified and detailed history of the involvement, sparked a little rebellion.

The war, he decided, was a wrongheaded and fraudulent undertaking. The American people had been continually deceived about its true nature and presidential leadership had avoided responsibility. The Harvard-educated Ellsberg began his rebellion, eventually joining a Rand colleague, Anthony J. Russo, Jr., by duplicating the papers for reporter Neil Sheehan of the *Times*; the newspaper defied their classified status and began to make them public in mid-June 1971. The account was melancholy, a catalogue of mistakes and deceptions.

Every event described predated the Nixon presidency. He could have remained aloof and enjoyed what was essentially internecine warfare among Democrats, as some aides suggested, but Nixon debated whether to act to prevent their publication. The American *heartland*, they argued, was not interested in such academic carping anyway, and it would soon be forgotten.

Those were the gut arguments that continued to float during the weeks after the papers were published. As he contemplated a response, he became more inclined to fire back at the Democrats. Additional reinforcement came at an Oval Office meeting on June 22 that included Henry Kissinger, along with his assistant, General Alexander Haig.

Nixon, finally won over by Kissinger's arguments and convinced that the Democrats would be the big losers, took the case to the Supreme Court, arguing that the First Amendment did not give newspapers the right to publish stolen classified government documents that had a bearing on the national interest. "If we did not move against the *Times*," he later wrote, "it would be a signal to every disgruntled bureaucrat in the government that he could leak anything he pleased while the government simply stood by."

Forty-five thousand Americans had already died in Vietnam. Coming when it did, just weeks after the May Day demonstration, their publication risked further aggravating the situation. The decision to enter the fight against the Pentagon Papers also enabled Nixon to take on both the press and the antiwar movement, scoring points with the public even if he lost in the Supreme Court, which he did, by a 6 to 3 split. About all that could be done with the press was to put them on guard, get them to overcompensate.

The sequence of events from that point on emphasized how alarmed the Nixon administration became over the adequacy of its own security. Ehrlichman's Plumbers now gathered power and significance. Funded by leftover campaign funds, and eventually supplemented by CREEP, its importance was underscored. Joining the unit to prevent leaks (hence the dubbing of "plumbers") and carry out other security missions was an attorney from Colson's staff, a zealous former prosecutor from Poughkeepsie in New York's Hudson Valley, G. Gordon Liddy, and an ex-CIA and Bay of Pigs veteran, E. Howard Hunt. With the evolution of the Plumbers, the activities of the White House's "security" measures escalated, and so did its preemptive strikes. Liddy and Hunt were okayed to use their connections to put together a "black-bag" team.

Ongoing antiwar demonstrations during the warm months of 1971 clearly joined with the Pentagon Papers affair to ignite the sense of alarm. Nothing made Nixon's passion for striking back at the students and radicals clearer than when he instructed Haldeman on June 30 to "just break in and take" what could be evidentiary material from a liberal think tank on Massachusetts Avenue, the Brookings Institution. "I want the break-in," said the president in the Oval Office. "You're to break into the place, rifle the files, and bring them in. . . . You go in to inspect the safe. I mean, *clean it up.*" Nothing came of that, although there was discussion later about possibly firebombing Brookings. In early September, however, a forced entry did take place in the Los Angeles office of Dr. Fred Fielding, Ellsberg's psychiatrist. But it came to naught, a futile search requested by Ehrlichman to prove the mental instability of the man who exposed the Pentagon Papers.

Nixon, at about the same time, reacted to a complaint from the Rev. Billy Graham. The nation's best known clergyman told him that the IRS was investigating *his* tax records. Haldeman promptly recorded in his diary that the president's response included a demand for the White House "to get the names of the big Democratic contributors and get them investigated," along with the names of "Democratic celebrities and so forth." How they went about it, presumably, was up to them, but it was a presidential mission.

Then, as though to further justify having Plumbers, there was the Jack Anderson–Admiral Moorer affair. Anderson, a muckraking prominent newspaper columnist, published revelations about the administration's diplomatic attitude toward the 1971 conflict between India and Pakistan. Far from being evenhanded during the crisis, as official reports indicated, Anderson's filched documents showed the opposite: Nixon actually supported Pakistan. Through the Plumbers, the president learned that the columnist's information had come directly from the office of the Joint Chiefs of Staff (JCS). A young stenographer, Yeoman Charles Radford, had stolen "eyes only" information for the benefit of the JCS chairman, Admiral Thomas H. Moorer, who leaked it to Anderson. "This creates a highly sensitive situation," recorded Haldeman in his diary. The president prudently never pressed his case against the admiral, his hands tied because of the information already in their possession. Nixon, not ruffling anything, reappointed Moorer to another term as JCS chairman. Radford, the naval stenographer, was shipped off to a recruiting station in Oregon.

* * *

With the problem of re-election looming, Spiro Agnew's role had to be recast. Nixon preferred having Agnew step down before the election season. Then, using the Twenty-fifth Amendment, he could nominate John Connally and replace him in line as his successor to the presidency. Although a Democrat, Connally was a good conservative governor of Texas and a reliable Nixon ally, the kind of "tough son of a bitch" he admired. Moreover, getting rid of Agnew and replacing him with Connally belonged to Nixon's party realignment scheme. Connally, Nixon was also assured, would be part of "a populist, new Republican position." But Connally was not very interested.

Given Agnew's following and the Wallace threat, dumping him did not make much sense; that soon became apparent. Conservatives were restless. Nixon's requests that spring to his staff for clarifications of his programs showed his concern about moving toward the right. The administration was pushing its Family Assistance Plan [FAP], that was still widely regarded as a "guaranteed annual income" and continuing to fund such Great Society holdovers as the Office of Economic Opportunity. In January 1971, Nixon's State of the Union message proclaiming his "New American Revolution" had called for "revolutionary" programs in the areas of health, the environment, and the means of achieving a full employment economy. That summer, "draft Reagan" drives became general, and a noted conservative voice, William F. Buckley, Jr., declared that he had gone about as far as he could with the administration. Pollster Lou Harris later noted that while 52 percent of Americans favored replacing the vice president, Republicans wanted him to remain. Agnew clearly had to stay in order "to satisfy the Right."

Connally's role, meanwhile, was far from over. He became a prime force, if not *the* major force, in steering Nixon and his team toward acceptance of wage and price controls. The problem was twofold: continued rising inflation and a drain on gold through the international markets. The Texas Democrat suggested a high-level meeting at Camp David in mid-August of 1971, and it was Connally who used the phase "closing the gold window" to describe their actions on convertibility. The United States no longer would, because it no longer could, keep open the "window" to allow the dollar to be exchanged for gold at the fixed price of $35 an ounce in international trade. Out of that three-day session at Camp David, in the Catoctin Mountains of Maryland, came the astonishing news that conservative Republicans, of all people, had imposed a system of controls on prices and wages.

That was the great Nixon turnabout in fiscal matters. In reality, his flexibility had been signaled earlier. After the 1970 elections, he remarked that "I am now a Keynesian," which meant that the economics of full employment was to get priority over budget balancing. Nevertheless, the men around him were, in effect, locked away from the rest of the world. They were traditional free market conservatives.

Faced with the reality of the international monetary situation, however, and combined with the president's need to do something to demonstrate both at home and abroad that action was being taken, they capitulated. "We need action," Nixon told them; "inflation robs the working man. He's on a treadmill."

The gold window and convertibility problem was one thing, but whether that required the phased imposition of controls was another question. Controls were seen as insurance—included for psychological reasons—against a chaotic disruption of the world markets. Burns himself, in arguing against convertibility, had feared pandemonium and chaos on Wall Street.

Traditional free-market conservatives never forgave Nixon. To them, it symbolized an abandonment of any convictions, a catering to political expediency. They liked to point out that lifting the phased system of controls removed the lid from the upward pressures and, during the last two years of his administration, prices shot upward. For administration cynics, such as his head of the Council of Economic Advisers, it made sense only as a political move.

* * *

Jack Anderson went right on poking. "There's a building story again on the reopening of the Howard Hughes loan," Haldeman noted on January 17, 1972. The problem, Dean soon verified, was that Anderson's investigators had uncovered information that the columnist was "looking for information on the Hughes loan to Don Nixon," the president's brother. Dean had also listened to Liddy present a hair-brained scheme for sabotaging the Democratic national nominating convention scheduled for Miami Beach in the summer, a scenario that made the pipe-puffing attorney general, Mitchell, wince. The proposal, which included supplying the Democratic delegates with planted prostitutes, was too weird, but not sufficiently way-out not to emerge as a reincarnation called Operation Gemstone.

On February 8, Anderson reported in the *Washington Post* that "At almost the same time that Howard Hughes gave a $205,000 loan to Richard Nixon's brother [Donald], the Internal Revenue Service reversed itself and granted Hughes a tax break worth millions."

If the press was at war against the president, he was at war with them. As a Nixon aide put it to Haldeman in late April, "the discrediting of the press must be our major objective over the new few months," meaning, of course, during the pre-election period. He urged his chief of staff to find someone to carry out that assignment. Turning to Colson, Haldeman explained that "It is the national television and press media, based in Washington, not the media in the country. . . . their total support of ultra-liberal causes and their deliberate distortion of reporting as distinguished from editorializing on news events."

* * *

After three years of quiet contacts between the U.S. and China, the summit conference that became the most spectacular diplomatic event of the Nixon presidency, really kicked off in the spring of 1971 when the regime in Peking (now Beijing) invited a touring United States table tennis team to participate in world championship matches. Chinese Premier Zhou Enlai personally received the team on April 14. What the Americans called "ping-pong" suddenly became a wedge to unfreeze Cold War diplomacy. The next day, Nixon chose Kissinger, not Secretary of State Rogers (who was not informed until Kissinger was en route to China), to make an exploratory trip to Peking—"exploratory," though it would later be described; it was highly classified at the time. Not only had "direct communication" been established, but plans were made for a future visit by Nixon himself.

On July 6, while his ambassador to the United Nations, George H. W. Bush, was resisting granting a seat to the Chinese Communists, the president made news from a meeting of news executives in Kansas City. The time had come, he said, when it was "essential" for the administration to "take the first step toward ending the isolation of Mainland China." With Ambassador Bush as much in the dark as the American public, Kissinger went to Peking in October, this time for substantive discussions on major world issues.

In February, the world saw something that would have been unthinkable a few years earlier. Dick and Pat, the targets of South American insurgents in 1958, were walking on top of the Great Wall of China. The president had just spent four hours with Zhou. Merely seeing the two together was a significant breakthrough, and no one was more appreciative of its importance than Nixon. "When our hands met," wrote Nixon, "one era ended and another began." In the cold of that winter day, wearing a fur-collared coat, the president said, "As we look at this wall, what is most important is that we have an open world."

The symbolic highlight—and symbolism was dominant—came when Nixon met with Mao Zedong, the ideological and political leader of some one billion Chinese. Nixon soon learned what the outside world did not know, that the chairman was beset with bronchitis and barely able to talk, which, Zhou had warned in advance, would limit their session to about ten minutes. But they went on for nearly a full hour.

The chairman reached out his hand to shake Nixon's, which the president later described as "probably the most moving moment." Mao also said that he had "voted" for

Nixon shaking hands with Chairman Mao Zedong in Beijing, China
© Corbis

Nixon in the last election. Undoubtedly, the president responded jocularly, that must have been because he was
"the lesser of the two evils."

"I like rightists," answered Mao. Nixon, not losing the
moment, replied in a more serious manner by saying, "I
think the most important thing to note is that in America,
at least at this time, those on the right can do what those
on the left can only talk about."

"The Chinese Army band played 'America the Beauti-
ful' and 'Home on the Range,'" noted the euphoric *New
York Times*. It looked more like a "reunion of old friends
rather than the first social meeting of the leaders of two
nations that have been bitterly hostile for more than two
decades."

After eight days of meetings, sightseeing, and drinking, and after sitting through a tedious three-hour ballet, the American president left exchanging pledges for the gradual increase in American-Chinese contacts. The United States also promised to begin to withdraw American forces from Formosa, Peking's chief irritant. In a joint communiqué worked out over several days and issued after they got to Shanghai, they declared, among other provisions pledging comity that neither the U.S. nor the People's Republic of China "should seek hegemony in the Asia Pacific region and each is opposed to efforts by any other country or group of countries to establish such hegemony." The Shanghai Communiqué, as it came to be known, Nixon later wrote, "made it clear that we both would oppose efforts by the USSR or any other major power to dominate Asia." In a final toast before he departed, the president said, "The joint communiqué which we have issued today will change the world."

Thus, Nixon concluded the finest week of his presidency. A historic, if incremental, normalization of relations between the two countries had begun. It became obvious to point out that his own history as an anti-Chinese Communist hard-liner had enabled him not only to get away with the move; except for the shock to hard-line conservatives in his own country, he was heavily applauded by the American public. The "China opening" remained the most popular single act of his presidency, especially welcome in the months leading up to the elections. What had been "Red China" became to Nixon and to the State Department thereafter the People's Republic of China, followed by a boost in American public opinion toward its nearly three-decade-old adversary.

For the Americans to go on ignoring "Red" China was inherently unproductive, made more so by the additional complication of seeing the Vietnamese war as necessary to counter their expansionist ambitions. The Chinese, who boasted of their Marxist purity in contrast to the Soviets, were major suppliers of Ho Chi Minh's forces. Their involvement was essential if any solutions were to be found to what Kissinger has described as the "agony of Vietnam." "For twenty years," he wrote, "U.S. policymakers considered China as a brooding, chaotic, fanatical, and alien realm difficult to comprehend and impossible to sway."

The irony, of course, is that Nixon, as a certified hardliner, had more latitude to act. His reconsideration of American policy was encouraged by the French and West German leaders, who argued that Communist China was too big to be ignored, too vital for the United States to play a role in Asia without them; the Chinese were also sensitive to the history of abuse at the hands of Western colonial powers. Nixon began to understand that, without relating to Peking, Washington's efforts to achieve a settlement in Vietnam would continue to be frustrated. He also appreciated the depth of the schism between Peking and Moscow. His talks with Pakistani and Filipino leaders indicated that the Chinese were turning around and that a different relationship should be sought. His 1967 article in *Foreign Affairs* was an important early expression of that kind of thinking. When he was charged with deception about a "secret plan" during the 1968 campaign, he really did have in mind a regional solution; not only what came to be known as Vietnamization but also the China initiative. For all Nixon's reasons to create such an opening, it took Peking's apprehension about Soviet intentions to jump-start the process.

There were, in addition, too many other complicating factors in the region: commercial relations, nationalism, and concerns about Japan all the way to the Asian subcontinent. Any influence in the area inevitably involved the People's Republic, so Nixon insisted in a later interview that the war "was not the only reason I undertook the rapprochement with China. Had there been no Vietnam War, we would have had to seek new relations with China. We had to move in that direction. Nobody in a responsible position could fail to seek such a new relationship."

At the same time, it was a flirtation of convenience. The Chinese had to play their "American card." They were worried about any future revival of militarism in their old nemesis, Japan, and fearful of the threat from their ideological competitor, the Soviet Union. Moscow was in uncomfortable rapport with Washington, a consequence of the Kennedy initiatives on atmospheric nuclear testing and Johnson's opening of a dialogue about limiting strategic weapons.

The highly publicized trip, the pictures of him on the Great Wall, visiting the Forbidden City, drinking champagne with Zhou, were invaluable for casting Nixon in the light in which he had always wanted to be seen, as a statesman. When the trip was first announced, the president's top aides were scarcely able to conceal their glee about what it would do to the Democrats. When he returned to Washington, he told the large welcoming crowd that the visit had established "the basis of a structure for peace" without sacrificing the interests of America's allies.

The nation was delighted. What it really meant for the long run was, of course, unknown; but a start had been made. It was also, in a real sense, a step toward the restoration of the historic "special relationship" between the two countries. The years since 1949 had been an aberration. The old conditioning, which included longstanding solicitude toward the Chinese people, especially when they were seen as victims of Japanese aggression, was permitting a dilution of the "China syndrome." Nixon used that relationship to make it possible.

But the political payoff was not entirely to the president's satisfaction. The press was too diverted by such trivialities as the panda story; they could hardly wait to "bring up a negative point like the Rogers-Kissinger dispute" commanding the presidential ear in the making of foreign policy. "We cannot assume that there is a significant lasting effect of even such a great event as the China trip," the president noted for Haldeman's consumption. Gains, however, were recorded; after registering barely stronger than his potential Democratic rivals before the trip and with fear of Muskie as the most likely opponent, approval ratings in March showed him at 59 percent.

It also cast him in the role of a centrist or opportunist instead of a hard-line conservative. "We've agreed that we will not negotiate the fate of other nations behind their backs," he said, and other critics worried that he had indeed done just that: He had signaled to our Pacific allies, especially Japan, that the Nixon Doctrine really meant a reduction in overall military support for the region. The *National Review's* Bill Buckley deplored the loss of "any remaining sense of moral mission in the world." Nevertheless, Nixon, when he studied the results of the New Hampshire primary less than two weeks after his return, decided that there was no evidence that it had done much to sway Republican voters. Even more keenly disappointed, if for other reasons, was Secretary Rogers, who complained to the president soon afterward that the China trip upgraded Dr. Kissinger over the State Department.

But Rogers was not in the cabinet for the purpose of designing foreign policy. He was the president's loyal friend and a good negotiator. Kissinger was the idea man. As Nixon said at Camp David later that year, Kissinger was a "rag merchant" who started by bargaining at 50 percent to get to 25 percent. "That's why he's so good with the Russians."

Later, after the Yom Kippur War in 1973, Kissinger made headlines for his "shuttle diplomacy" in the Middle

East, working between the Arabs and the Israelis toward a policy far less evenhanded than Rogers and the State Department desired, and became the administration's all-star glamour boy. It was inevitable, given Rogers's growing chagrin at all this, that he would soon drop out of the team and that the German-Jewish refugee with an accent as thick as his glasses would take over the State Department. Rogers's pride constantly clashed with the duplicitous Kissinger. In his later memoir of his years with Nixon, Kissinger continued to diminish the man who preceded him as secretary of state. Rogers, on his part, never overcame his bitterness, not only toward his rival but toward his old friend, Nixon.

* * *

At the same time, the Wallace candidacy posed its own dangers. In the ongoing primaries, the segregationist Alabaman was doing predictably well in the South by finishing first in Florida's Democratic primary after emphasizing his opposition to busing. However regional certainties may have encouraged the minimization of that outcome, McGovern, while campaigning in Wisconsin, expressed surprise over the "despair in this country" provoked by the desegregation movement. As though to underscore McGovern's alarm, the Wisconsin outcome demonstrated Wallace's power north of the Mason-Dixon Line. He finished second in a six-man field, behind only McGovern and ahead of such Democratic powers as Humphrey and Muskie. While the Wisconsin primary did, ultimately, show McGovern's strength in the fight for the Democratic nomination, the segregationist's competition was not lost on Nixon. Further evidence came out of Pennsylvania three weeks later. Wallace, picking up sizable support from labor, placed second in that primary, 14 percentage points behind the leader, Humphrey, and one point ahead of McGovern. Even more emphatic than Wallace's accomplishment in Wisconsin, his subsequent clear victory in Michigan underscored blue collar discontent with "forced busing." For all the heralding of Wallace as a savior of the South, he could no longer be minimized as a mere regional candidate. He had, in fact, outstripped his rivals in total primary votes with 3.4 million to Humphrey's 2.7 million and McGovern's 2.2 million.

The president, ever wary of Wallace, never relaxed his opposition to transporting children by bus outside of their own districts to effectuate school desegregation. In meetings with congressional leaders in mid-February, he gave assurances that he would act to offset recent federal decisions requiring such means, even if he had to find a "constitutional route." Little wonder, then, that such papers as the *Miami Herald* exulted with this kind of headline: "They're Whistlin' for Nixon in Dixie."

Then there was the collapse of Muskie, the odds-on early favorite. Nixon's Committee to Re-Elect the President had the sabotaging of the respected Democratic senator as a major goal, and so he became the victim of pranks financed by CREEP. The "dirty tricks" included a bogus letter alleging that Jane Muskie, the senator's wife, had laughingly said that while Maine did not have blacks, "we have 'Cannocks [sic].'" William Loeb, the vitriolic right-wing publisher of New Hampshire's most influential newspaper, the *Manchester Union Leader*, ran the letter together with an editorial that contained the flat statement, "Sen. Muskie Insults Franco-Americans."

On February 26, just over a week before the key New Hampshire primary, Muskie stood on a flatbed truck before Loeb's newspaper office in downtown Manchester amid falling snow and became emotional while defending his wife from the falsehood. Images went out to the country of tears running down his face along with melting snowflakes. Seen over and over again on television and constantly described in the press, the images shattered Muskie's standing, especially when contrasted with the pictures of Nixon standing on the Great Wall in China. Muskie nevertheless won that primary, by a 46 to 37 percent edge. Still, it was seen as a disappointing performance for one whose political base was in the adjacent state of Maine.

Coming out of that two-man contest, McGovern's field was relatively clear from then on. Neither Kennedy nor Muskie stood in his way. McGovern, more in the tradition of William Jennings Bryan than of anyone the nation had recently seen, had become the ideal of the reformist "New Politics" movement, in effect, the political arm of the counterculture. His anti–Vietnam War passions drew legitimacy from his military record as the holder of a Distinguished Flying Cross and veteran of more than 35 missions over Germany, Austria, and Italy during the great war against the Nazis. He spoke with moral conviction, and, enroute to the nomination by his party for the presidency, he was aided by the new delegate selection process and carrying a message that resonated with reformist Democrats. McGovern was their clear choice.

A McGovern concoction, announced in January as a "demogrant" that would provide a $1,000 annual payment to every man, woman, and child in America, finally doomed what little life remained in Nixon's Family Assistance Plan (FAP). Nixon's scheme, already wracked about by conservatives as well as liberals, suffered from even a faint association with McGovern's. When the president met with the cabinet at Camp David in April, three months after the birth of McGovern's plan, he suggested what to do with FAP. "Flush it," he said. "Blame it on the budget." Nixon's advisers agreed that with McGovern and the Democrats on the left, it ill-behooved the administration to move toward the center.

Later, in a 1988 interview, he offered the following explanation for dropping FAP:

> Oh, I know it [abandoning FAP] was necessary, in order to keep the country together and to keep the coalition together. Politically, I wasn't going to pick up by reason of my support of FAP, by reason of my support of the Philadelphia Plan, by reason of my impeccable civil rights record, by reason of my minority business things, all of which were progressive ideas. I knew that I wasn't going to pick up a substantial number of the liberal Democrats, the black Democrats, et cetera. I knew that wasn't going to happen. . . . I had to at least take positions that the liberals didn't like. The liberals have a litmus test: you've got to be all for us or you're against us.

On May 15, at a shopping center rally in Laurel, Maryland, just north of the nation's capital, a bullet fired by a young drifter effectively removed George Wallace from contention. The crippling of the Alabama governor, Nixon later emphasized, did not kill his ideas. Kissinger's military assistant, General Haig, was promptly designated as "a sort of liaison" to Wallace. His explicit instructions included ensuring the ex-governor that the president was very strongly opposed to busing, as indicated on the Republican platform.

If the Democrats were ready to go with McGovern, which was especially indicated by the Dakotan's vote in states where delegates were chosen through conventions rather than primaries, thanks to new selection rules put in place by reformers, they were doomed from the start, about to select someone trailing Nixon in "trial-heat" election polls.

10

A "Third-Rate" Burglary

Three months after the Peking trip, on May 22, 1972, Nixon arrived in Moscow. He scored another triumph and became the first American president to visit the Russian capital. The diplomacy in Moscow was the culmination of a process begun during the Johnson presidency. The road to negotiations about détente began with LBJ's warning to Soviet Premier Kosygin that the deployment of an antiballistic missile defense system around Moscow had created pressures within the United States "to increase greatly our capabilities to penetrate any defensive systems which you might establish." Both countries proceeded to a treaty banning the spread of nuclear weapons to countries that did not have any and were ready to go on to talks about limiting offensive and defensive strategic weapons. Then, in August 1968, came the Soviet invasion of Czechoslovakia and, with it, an end to any further progress. Along with Nixon's inauguration, the Soviet Foreign Ministry, apparently eager to revive the arms limitation process, invited Washington for a resumption of talks. That led to the opening of what has been called SALT I, a half-year series of negotiations that wound up with Nixon visiting Moscow.

Accompanied by both Rogers and Kissinger, he was received by Communist Party Secretary General Leonid I.

Brezhnev and Premier Aleksey N. Kosygin. The greeting was subdued, unlike the Peking reception, less because of the U.S.–China opening than because of the recent bombing of the North Vietnamese capital of Hanoi and the port at Haiphong. The Soviets claimed that four of its ships were hit.

The sessions then got down to continuing the effort to cap the arms race and followed through on the Helsinki openings about strategic weapons. The Moscow summit ended with Nixon and Brezhnev signing a series of historic documents in the Great Hall of the Kremlin.

Most important was the antiballistic missile treaty (ABM Treaty). Limits had never before been placed on the growth of American and Soviet strategic missile arsenals. Seen at the time as a mere beginning, it was, nevertheless, a major gain in the long history of nuclear arms control legislation, freezing in place the recent Soviet buildup; a step had been taken toward the elusive goal of disarmament. The two leaders acted to boost grain sales to the Soviet Union, with the U.S. following through by extending $750 million for their purchases over the next three years.

Most significant perhaps was the assumption that deterrence would remain most effective so long as superior offensive weapons made each superpower vulnerable to massive retaliation. More important than the actual accomplishments was keeping the dialogue alive, and the ability to go on despite what was happening in Vietnam. Or, to put it another way, relationships with both Peking and Moscow did have something to do with the fighting in Vietnam.

On May 24, Nixon met with Brezhnev at the Soviet leader's dacha. The president then threw one of his "long balls," a diplomatic effort to get the Russians to help him get out of Vietnam.

"You say you want to end this war and quite calmly put forward the idea. But this is at a time when you are carrying out . . . a different effort to destroy a country and kill off thousands, millions of innocent people. . . . But how can the methods you use now be called a method of ending the war in Vietnam?" Brezhnev retorted.

Nixon must have realized the resemblance of such words to Khrushchev's lecture to Kennedy in Vienna in 1961. "This is just a small war," he said in response. "But it has cost the U.S. 50,000 dead and 200,000 wounded. . . . We are trying by a simple cease-fire to end the war—in other words, to impose a peace."

Nixon left that encounter no less frustrated than had Kennedy from his meeting a decade earlier. Both leaders had agreed on the need for a reciprocal visit in 1973. Neither of the two major Communist powers, Nixon was finding out, would help to ease his way out of Vietnam.

The United States–Soviet dialogue naturally made Peking nervous and helped to move them toward playing *their* "American card." As the Chinese declared, "The United States–Soviet talks on so-called 'strategic arms limitations' are aimed at further developing their nuclear military alliance. They mainly hope to maintain a nuclear monopoly and carry out nuclear blackmail by nuclear threats against the Chinese people and the people of the world." Ultimately, Nixon's triangular diplomacy, shrewdly taking advantage of the mutual discomfiture of two rival states, moved the great powers toward a turning point in the Cold War. Thus, clearly, he approached reelection as a statesman searching for world peace.

* * *

Although he had been out of the administration since May, John Connally was very much a part of the Nixon campaign. He became head of Democrats for Nixon, the next best thing to having him replace Agnew on the ticket; in fact, it was a better idea. Nixon could then have both.

Connally and Nixon, recalled Ehrlichman, had many conversations before the 1972 conventions about getting more Democrats on board, the left-wing "theft" of the party presumably simplifying the process, the elimination of the Wallace factor freeing him from wooing populism. Now he was engaged in building a coalition that would occupy, said Ehrlichman, the "broadest part of the middle—all of the South and most of the North, leaving to the liberals what was left." Had Watergate not interfered, Connally calculated, the odds for the success of realignment would have been about fifty-fifty.

Their projected realignment, aimed at reshaping the Republican Party, sought to embrace southern leadership. Republicans could become competitive in the region despite the Democratic hold on grassroots levels. Connally assumed that successful realignment would have kept the Republican Party from shifting to the far right by attracting a vast pool of conservative Democrats who were not, "in any sense," said Connally, "philosophical radicals." The planned re-grouping within the GOP would, hopefully, be biracial and attractive to middle-class whites and blacks from all regions of the country.

Connally was a very persuasive fellow. Liberals thought of him as a high-flying robber baron Texas gambler who rolled in millions. He was tarnished for a time by an alleged involvement in milk price-fixing but finally acquitted, all of which had little to do with Big John's clout. He started out poor and made fortunes through close involvement with the oil and gas industry. The self-made image was, of course, irresistible to Nixon. Connally, someone once said, was "LBJ with couth."

Associates within the administration could respect all that. But people like Treasury Secretary William Simon regarded Connally as a populist, which was *exactly how Connally viewed Nixon.*

* * *

Nixon and his people, confident about winning a second term, had become sufficiently conditioned by political insecurity to be on guard about taking success for granted. On the advice of his chief conservative speechwriter, Pat Buchanan, as well as Colson, he reached out to some of the traditionally most reliable Democrats, working-class Catholics. He delivered a stroke in that direction most deftly in early May with the release of his letter to Terence Cardinal Cooke of New York, supporting the Cardinal's fight to repeal the state's permissive abortion laws. Releasing the letter to the press dispelled any doubt about what the Nixon people had in mind. "I would personally like to associate myself with the convictions you deeply feel and eloquently express," explained the Nixon letter. On June 8, after the virtual elimination of the wounded Wallace and following McGovern's triumph over Humphrey in California's key winner-take-all primary, Buchanan advised, tellingly, that McGovern "is outside the power elite of the Democratic Party; he is perceived as outside the power elite of the American government." He should be attacked by appealing to issues strongly favored by Catholics, opponents of racial integration, and those hostile toward the media. In other words, ran the advice, "we should increasingly portray McGovern as the pet radical of Eastern Liberalism, the darling of the *New York Times*. . . ." He should be identified as "Mr. Radical Chic," and be linked with "abortion, amnesty, pot, the removal of the personal tax exemption (a killer for large Catholic families) . . . in Catholic and ethnic areas, Catholic and ethnic papers, Catholic and ethnic forums." Moreover, Buchanan advised, he should also be tied to "black radical schemes." Nixon, only recently back from Russia, agreed. On June 10, he assured his speechwriter that "if you were to interview the working press traveling with McGovern, you would find that 90% of them agreed with his stand on amnesty [for draft-dodgers], pot, surrender in Vietnam confiscation of wealth, the $1000 baby bonus [McGovern's demogrants] for welfare recipients, etc. . . . The left wing's primary motivation is power." Another top Nixon speech writer, Bill Safire, noting that Humphrey had exposed the weakness of McGovern's support for Israel, suggested that the president utilize New York's Jewish Republicans instead of old-time Jews with their defeatist attitude about Nixon and the Jews. One New York City congressman, Ben Rosenthal, a Queens Democrat, pointed out that the "base of political reliability that existed ten, fifteen, twenty years ago isn't there anymore. The same low income groups, the same ethnic groups, the same intellectual-left oriented people are not under the same umbrella anymore. . . . The same conditions don't exist, the same unity of forces doesn't exist; the same unity of purpose doesn't exist."

Nixon, taking a cue from what his aides had laid out, took another giant step toward reshaping the Republican Party. He advised Colson and Haldeman of the obvious fact that Sergeant Shriver, who had replaced Thomas Eagleton as the Democratic vice presidential candidate, and McGovern, were going after the ethnic vote to rebuild the old Democratic coalition.

"They have read the polls," emphasized the president, "and they see that we have made these outstanding gains in the Catholic community and among the blue collar workers and labor generally. . . . We cannot assume that because we have moved up among Catholics and blue collar workers that that will hold. . . . That is why the use of [Frank] Rizzo [the mayor of Philadelphia], the Italian labor leaders who have moved with us, the Italian political leaders who have moved toward us, [Cardinal] Krol and the Polish group, etc., all of these are of very first priority this time"—another move by Nixon toward his new majority, with a stronger ethnic base that could beat back dominance by "elitists."

Interviewed by the author about a dozen years later, Nixon remained determined about his new majority. "Had we not been cut short we would have had a realignment of parties." His realigned group aimed at including middle-class blacks without taking "reactionary stands" on social issues, and with strong support for private enterprise and fiscal responsibility. All in all, his vision of a revamped Republican Party would attract professionals along with blue-collar groups. "The Republican Party is still elitist," he then added with some exasperation, obviously regretting a lost cause. He also confirmed his studied shift to the right after 1970.

But, in 1972, while composing the game book for that reelection campaign, the fact that his opposition was so heavily composed of "left-wing" McGovernites inspired his fulminations about the "decadent elitism" of his critics, who, after all, were pillars of the Establishment: the press, Ivy League colleges, and aristocratic professionals, a milieu that even included his own law school at Duke with its "many left-wing deans." "We must build a new establishment," Nixon told his aides at Camp David on March 21, 1972. "We must assume that the working press is the enemy. Fight them." "Our friends are local commentators and editors. A new establishment should be created in the press. People like Don Kendall of Pepsi-Cola, a good friend and supporter, a self-made businessman, got to the top without help from an Ivy League School." During a cabinet discussion, Nixon referred to Peter Brennan, who was about to become his secretary of labor, by pointing out that "only Brennan & I come from working class." A few weeks before the election, he told speechwriter Safire to take a crack at "this elitist business." You know, he went on, "that's why they don't like the ethnics, the people who use poor grammar—they believe that all that's required for leadership is education, but of course that's wrong. Leadership requires character, and too much education today destroys character."

Rampaging antiwar college students were exactly what he was talking about, overindulged, over-privileged, spoiled, too cowardly to fight for their country. Lift the threat of military service and see how much they would then care about the war. On August 28, after agreeing with Haldeman on the wisdom of acting before the presidential election, Nixon fulfilled a promise made during the 1968 campaign, announcing the end of mandatory conscription after July 1973. He gave the kids what he thought they were *really* after, but did away with a selective service system long under fire for its built-in escapes for the children of the wealthy and well connected, leaving the pathetic *grunts* to save the free world from communism.

He also moved ahead with the troop-withdrawal aspect of Vietnamization, and it worked. By barring Vietnam duty for new draftees and by reducing U.S. ground forces, he went far to dissipate continued agitation at home.

* * *

The two-year route to Nixon's ultimate downfall began during the night of June 17, 1972, when five "burglars" were caught breaking into Larry O'Brien's offices at the Democratic National Committee located in the Watergate complex of luxury apartments and commercial establishments on Washington's Virginia Avenue. Caught red-handed and fully equipped with a walkie-talkie, photographic and recording devices, especially the capability for bugging telephone and room conversations, as well as tools for turning lock cylinders, they were nevertheless at first put down by Nixon's press secretary, Ron Ziegler, as "third-rate burglars."

Hardly "third rate," they all had some ties to intelligence organizations, Liddy under Hoover in the FBI, and Hunt with the CIA. Another ex-CIA man, James W. McCord, who had broken into the Democratic headquarters two weeks earlier to install a telephone bug, ran security operations for both the Republican National Committee and CREEP. Among those also arrested, taken at gunpoint that night thanks to a keen-eyed building guard, Frank Wills, were anti-Castro Cubans led by Bernard L. Barker, a veteran of CIA planning for the Bay of Pigs. Another "burglar" involved in that disastrous Kennedy-era attack was the American-born Frank Sturgis, a former Marine. Eugenio Martinez and Virgilio Gonzalez, both of whom were taken into the custody the night when the team had to return to the Watergate because the May 27 phone bug had malfunctioned, were also anti-Castro Cuban-Americans. The composition of the team offered enough reason to spur suspicions of CIA plotting. Especially conducive to such conspiracy suspicions was the growing unease by some conservatives, including within the military establishment, about Nixon's pursuit of détente with the two major communist powers, let alone embracing Great Society reforms at home.

Few Americans noted the incident. If reported at all, it appeared as one or two back-page paragraphs, an isolated misdemeanor in the nation's capital. An exception was the *New York Times*, which did break out with a page-one story on June 19 that revealed the names and backgrounds of the men, obviously helped by the District of Columbia police's quick uncovering of evidence in room 214 of the Howard Johnson Motor Inn.

Nixon was on top of the news. The record, as ultimately developed, shows his early involvement in helping to orchestrate a cover-up. On June 21, he gave Haldeman assurances that "the reaction is going to be primarily

Washington and not the country," because the country couldn't care less about such things, "there than the ones we've already bugged." After all, they think that everybody's trying to bug everybody else. They don't give a damn about "repression and bugging and all the rest." Significant or not, thanks to the evidence found in the motel, little time was lost in connecting the break-in to the White House, which accentuated the significance of the break-in.

"Nixon *knew* what had happened," Haldeman was told after the incident. Ehrlichman, in the first of his two post-Watergate accounts, states flatly, "Richard Nixon, himself, caused those burglars to break into O'Brien's office." Thirty-one years later, in a surprising revelation, former White House aide, Jeb Stuart Magruder, who had remained mum on the subject, stated on a PBS documentary that he was at a meeting with Mitchell on March 30, 1972, when he caught Nixon's end of his phone conversation telling the attorney general to go ahead with the plan. Then, one year after the break-in, there was the early morning phone call from Martha Mitchell, the irascible and often irrepressible wife of the attorney general. To one of her press contacts, Helen Thomas, Mrs. Mitchell said, "I'll be damned if I'll let my husband take the rap for Mr. President." Then she added, "Between you and me and the gatepost, Mr. President always knew what was going on."

As hard as they tried in those remaining weeks before the presidential election, the McGovern Democrats failed to make the incident a major campaign issue. Public opinion remained unimpressed, with most grandly dismissing the incident as "just politics." Washington was far more of a problem to Washington insiders, those who enjoyed "inside baseball," than to the rest of the country. Only 48 percent of the public, according to Gallup, had even heard about the break-in, and the role of CREEP was basically moot.

A succession of almost daily headlines, most dramatically and tellingly in the *Washington Post* by reporters Bob Woodward and Carl Bernstein, revealed campaign operations involving break-ins, sabotage, fabrication of news stories and other "dirty tricks"—including one that helped to knock out Muskie as Nixon's rival—together with accounts of CREEP payments for so-called "hush" money. The stories first appeared in the *Post* on October 10, less than a month before Election Day, and went on to become a landmark in the history of American investigative journalism. The journalists later identified their major source as an individual they called Deep Throat (much later identified as Mark Felt of the FBI), a name inspired by a well-known pornographic movie of the time.

In that atmosphere, the president confidently pondered the development of a "thorough game plan" for Watergate. He was determined to "tough it out." The mantra was "protect the presidency," an objective reiterated constantly until the very end. As early as June 23, less than a week after the break-in, he told Haldeman that he wanted the CIA to keep the FBI from investigating. Acting director Pat Gray, who succeeded the retired Hoover, should be called by CIA deputy director Vernon Walters, Nixon said, and told to "Stay the hell out of this. . . . we don't want you to go any further on it."

* * *

Nixon's renomination machinery, unlike the operation of his hapless Democratic opponent, George McGovern, had only one problem. Not until April did the Republicans decide to also take their show to Miami Beach. The original commitment of some $400,000 from the International Telephone and Telegraph Company to select San Diego, and the Justice Department's subsequent dropping of an antitrust suit against ITT, constituted a scandal with little lasting effect. Miami Beach, Republicans then pointed out, was on a sand bar, thereby simplifying the problem of providing security against potential rioters.

The convention that followed after its August 21 opening was strictly a public relations gala rather than a nominating session. The ticket of President Richard Nixon and Vice President Spiro Agnew was renamed by acclamation. Unlike the mismanaged and chaotic Democratic convention, all was well orchestrated; a carefully prepared script detailed the precise times for each step. Speakers were cued when to pause, when to accept cheers, even when one speech was to be interrupted in mid-sentence for a "spontaneous" demonstration. Nixon's nomination was set for 10:33, to be followed by an equally "spontaneous" release of balloons.

For that fraction of the public that followed the unraveling of Watergate from its very beginnings, McGovern labored to exploit the issue throughout the fall. Various polls showed that most Americans had neither heard about Watergate nor, if they had, thought of it as a mere indulgence of the President's re-election committee. The stories of White House improprieties were, in any event, hardly enough to stop most Americans from safeguarding the republic by keeping conduct of the Vietnam War and the best interests of national security out of the hands of McGovern and his "radical" followers.

Nixon, in effect, went on that fall to take a cue from the FDR campaign of 1940 by acting aloof from politicking. Over a year and a half earlier, CREEP had selected and briefed 35 surrogates so that the president could remain in the White House, monitor the war and track Kissinger's peacemaking efforts with Saigon and Hanoi, and simply look "presidential." The separation of CREEP from the Republican National Committee effectively divorced the president's personal re-election interests from the needs of the party.

The war clearly boosted Nixon's re-election prospects. In May, he ordered the mining and bombing of Haiphong and military targets in North Vietnam. By August, the Harris studies showed the public had little confidence in McGovern's terms for peacemaking. By 49 to 33 percent, Americans banked that Nixon rather than the antiwar senator could achieve an earlier and better disengagement.

In Vietnam, intensification was, in part, a response to new enemy offensives and in preparation for a further withdrawal of American troops. But the fighting had been going on for a long time, throughout nearly the full length of Nixon's term, despite his election as the man who could end it.

Finally, after months of delicate secret negotiations, Kissinger announced that peace was "at hand." Kissinger's words came on October 26, 1972, less than two weeks before Election Day. Nixon and South Vietnam's leadership were both driving a hard bargain. Nixon's diplomacy, however, was more complicated. He had to achieve his goal by forcing the enemy to agree to terms by bludgeoning "Thieu into submission." Not even an additional $1 billion worth of military hardware was enough to move the South Vietnamese leader. Thieu, for his part, remained skeptical about his American allies, who, he knew, could desert him at any time. The reality, of course, was that Nixon was not about to defy Republican hawks just before the election; the man "who lost Vietnam" were about the last words he wanted to hear.

Having Kissinger release the "peace" statement, however, Nixon finally agreed, could not hurt. It was risk-free, its political timing reminiscent of the Nixon-backed effort to stall the peace talks in Paris before the 1968 election. Both Nixon and Kissinger had assumed from the start of their governance that "victory" in Vietnam was, in Nixon's word, "impossible." If nothing else, the statement could at least take the wind out of any effort by the McGovernites to further exploit the "peace issue" before Americans went to vote. Kissinger's message was even useful enough for Nixon himself to virtually repeat his words that same day while stumping in West Virginia and Kentucky by saying "There has been a breakthrough in the negotiations." Later, in a November 2 speech to the nation, with words drafted by Kissinger, Nixon remarked about "a major breakthrough toward achieving our goal of peace with honor in Vietnam."

While Thieu was trying to preserve South Vietnam, a specific set of agreements was still lacking. Nixon continued to stand behind the South Vietnamese leader while Hanoi reneged on some vital concessions that appeared to have been made earlier. Thieu's gambit was to keep the war going by disrupting any possible Hanoi-Washington accord, whereas Nixon was concerned that the peace, when it came, would be "with honor," implying future political acceptance. A premature cop-out risked resembling a McGovern-style settlement. American forces not only had to pull out, but their reason for having fought in the first place had to be secured. At least, Haldeman reminded him, the promise of peace, deceptive as it was, managed to upstage Watergate on the front pages. The incident also highlighted the tendency by Kissinger and Nixon to consider each other "paranoid." Kissinger, in Nixon's view, had grabbed the headlines and was "getting the play." Their jockeying for position sometimes resembled the Nixon-Kissinger atmospherics.

* * *

The Nixon administration had already done its utmost to intimidate both the print and electronic media; the possible underreporting of the early Watergate stories may have been the most significant consequence. While the

Republican candidate was endorsed by the overwhelming number of newspapers, McGovern received most of his support from the so-called "Eastern Liberal Press." The reduced importance of print in the popular dissemination of information was somewhat offset by the tendency of key newspapers to influence the agenda for television reporting.

In retrospect, it almost seems surprising that Nixon lost even one state. Massachusetts, along with the District of Columbia, gave McGovern a total of 17 electoral votes. Nixon's 60.7 percent share, which represented 47,167,319 popular votes to McGovern's 29,168,509, was second only to Lyndon Johnson's 61.1 percent in 1964.

More significant for the long run were the outlines of realignment. At least for the moment, both political parties were more deeply polarized. The clearest change was confirmation that, in presidential elections, the Republicans had reversed history and acquired a lock on the South, winning with Wallace out of the race—an improbable 70 percent of its popular votes. Nixon's sweep in the rest of the nation gave equally dramatic evidence of the change. He got the votes of slightly more than half of those who belonged to labor unions. He became the first Republican to win a majority of the Catholic vote, and he even cut into a sizable share of the Jewish and African-American vote that had gone to Humphrey in 1968. Nixon's commanding victory also broke the back of the great postwar New Deal–Fair Deal–Great Society era of American liberalism. Gone was his earlier signing on to LBJ's Great Society politics.

In the end, McGovern was more like Horace Greeley, the inept liberal Republican presidential candidate of 1872 than like William Jennings Bryan, the fiery "cross of gold" populist of 1896. It was Nixon who was perceived as the antiwar candidate, and, with Wallace out of the picture, it was also Nixon who made the populist appeal, albeit a conservative one. McGovern passed into popular lore as a disastrous fumbler, whose ineptitude handed a major victory to one of the most unpopular of major American politicians. His failure hurt the credibility of the reform movement.

Democrats ran best in states with the highest incomes, culture, education, health, welfare, and civil awareness, capturing, in effect, the civil rights constituency. Legislative success in behalf of minorities cost them the support of many who viewed government assistance to the disadvantaged as the sacrifice of white middle- and lower-class workers. Nothing established Nixon's conservative credentials as much as his vigorous opposition to busing. (One of his final presidential acts included the signing of a law passed by the Democratic Congress to prohibit the use of federal aid to pay for court-ordered busing.)

At first glance, how voters cast their ballots for congressional seats seems to be somewhat of an anomaly until one realizes that the pattern had, by then, become common. In 1972, in the face of the Nixon landslide, Democrats actually gained two Senate seats and Republicans picked up just 12 in the House, hardly a reflection of GOP strength on the local level. The presidency was clearly the most sensitive barometer of the national mood, which, by definition, left the Democrats in a wilderness they had not experienced since pre-New Deal days. Not even a flawless campaign could have won for McGovern.

Nixon versus McGovern divided the country along not only the so-called social issues, but also along ethnic, class, and cultural lines. The president had the support of such law-and-order Democrats as Philadelphia's mayor, Frank Rizzo, who ultimately became a Republican. En route to his 60 percent popular vote victory over McGovern, enough to win all electors outside the District of Columbia and Massachusetts, he made significant inroads among the middle- and working-classes who felt themselves alienated from the Democratic Party. Thus, a significant portion of the Wallace vote became Nixon's.

* * *

Nixon followed election day with one remaining bit of unfinished business. He meant not only to revamp the Republican party, but, having swept a strong re-election, he would make a commanding fresh start, destroying his enemies before they could destroy him. "I told Haldeman and Ehrlichman that I wanted an administration infused with the spirit of the 1972 New Majority," he recorded in his memoir. "I gave them four explicit criteria for selection: loyalty, breadth, creativity—and moxie. I wanted to appoint labor leaders, women, and members of ethnic groups, such as Poles, Italians, and Mexican Americans, that had not been adequately represented in the government in the past."

On November 8, with hardly enough time to thoroughly digest all the full implications of the election returns, he called for all non-career government employees of the executive branch, and then his cabinet as well, to submit their resignations. Striking utterly without warning, and conceived as a symbolic cleansing gesture, it nevertheless stunned loyalists who had labored for his re-election. One of his oldest hands, Herb Klein, has commented that the "act [was] the most disheartening, most surprising, and most cruel of all. . . . It was ungrateful and bitterly cold." Nixon himself, in his memoirs, concluded that it was a "mistake." As with the Swiss Guard incident, the move was a "mistake" when seen by the world. In the case of the sudden call for resignations, Nixon's act was incomprehensible on some levels, but, alas, consistent with the actions of a man whose life had become inseparable from the symbolism of the presidential seal. "I see this now as a mistake," Nixon later wrote. "I did not take into account the chilling effect this action would have on the morale of the people who had worked so hard during the election and who were naturally expected to savor a tremendous victory instead of suddenly having to worry about keeping their jobs."

On the day after the election, he told his national security adviser, Henry Kissinger, that the diplomatic corps needed a house-cleaning. They were, in Nixon's view, dominated by liberals, "cautious, unimaginative, slow-moving and risk-averse," as one State Department veteran put it. He would "ruin the Foreign Service. I mean ruin it," he assured Kissinger. Loyal appointees would be all around him. "The situation was compounded by my own isolation at Camp David, where I spent eighteen days in the four weeks after the election, holding more than forty meetings with old and new appointees and making plans for the second term," he wrote.

After his re-election, Nixon, without any public announcement, went straight for the kill. One week before Christmas, he explained in his diary, "We are on a tightrope here and I fear that as a result of the infiltration of the South Vietnamese that the North Vietnamese figure that they have us where the hair is short and are going to continue to squeeze us. That is why we had to take strong actions." He warned his top commander that it was his "chance to use military power to win this war, and if you don't, I'll consider you responsible." He would brook no "crap about the fact that we couldn't hit this target or that one."

Both Nixon and South Vietnam's president Nguyen Van Thieu were driving a hard bargain. In Hanoi, the North Koreans under Le Duc Tho were enjoying the sight of the Americans being held in virtual hostage by their clients in Saigon. With Kissinger and Al Haig as emissaries and Nixon banking on greater firmness from the latter, negotiations hinged on such matters as the mutual withdrawal of each side's troops, whether the demilitarized zone (DMZ) would serve as the boundary between North and South, and the return of prisoners of war (POWs). For Le Duc Tho, the revolutionary leader in close touch with the Soviets, the question was the likelihood of getting better terms after Nixon had been safely re-elected, knowing that the American president had to get out of the war one way or the other as long as it could be done "with honor."

Nixon's diary for December 9 contained the following entry: "The North wants to humiliate the South and us as well if possible. The South wants to drive the North out of South Vietnam and get us to stick with them until this goal is accomplished. As far as we are concerned, we must bring the war to an end on an honorable basis as quickly as possible."

Not stated, and never made very clear except to researchers of the peace process, was what Nixon considered a key obstacle to an armistice: Thieu, continuing to hold out, had to be convinced of the destruction of North Vietnam's military power. Nixon had even begun to contemplate another mission for Anna Chennault, this time to get Thieu to reconsider. Finally, after much back and forth bargaining, another rejection by the Communist leader convinced Nixon of the need for the "strongest action." His order of December 14 called for the reseeding of the mines in Haiphong Harbor, the resumption of aerial reconnaissance, and for B-52 bomber strikes at the North Vietnamese heart, the Hanoi-Haiphong complex.

Operation Linebacker II, the sequel to the Linebacker I bombing undertaken in the spring, had begun. Unleashed in the early morning hours of December 17, 129 B-52s participated in raids over North Vietnam within a 24-hour period. On December 20, 90 B-52s hit 11 targets, and 30 more sorties followed the next day against three new targets. The so-called "Christmas bombing," unloaded during a 12-day period, exceeded the power that had been used over the previous two years. It also struck some as the act of a "maddened tyrant," which was precisely Nixon's plan. Among the critics were the editorial writers of the *Washington Post*, who denounced it as "a bombing policy . . . so ruthless and so difficult to fathom politically as to cause millions of Americans to cringe in shame and to wonder at their President's very sanity."

As Nixon himself explained to Haldeman, "I call it the Madman Theory, Bob, I want the North Vietnamese to believe that I've reached the point where I might do *anything* to stop the war." He was, as he has acknowledged, fully conscious that "if the bombing did not succeed . . . there was no way of knowing how—or whether—the Vietnam War would end." Terror on the ground was exactly what he had intended. Meanwhile, outrage mounted at home. He had, suggested many critics, lost his sanity. Approval ratings dropped by 11 percent.

On the day after Christmas, following 116 additional B-52 sorties, the North Vietnamese had had enough and called for an end to what they called the "extermination bombing." All told, Nixon had directed a total of 3,420 bombings and support sorties, taking the lives of 2,196 civilians in Hanoi alone. The United States lost 12 percent of its B-52 bombers, and 121 crewmen were killed or became prisoners of war or were MIAs.

In the South, Thieu appeared to be mollified; his resistance softened. Kissinger and Le Duc Tho agreed to reopen the Parisian peace talks. The American need to disengage from the fighting was inevitable. Given written assurances of renewed military support if the Hanoi regime violated the truce terms and attempted to undermine the country, Thieu went along.

On January 23, 1973, Nixon announced the conclusion of "an agreement to end the war and bring peace with honor in Vietnam and South-east Asia." As he later recorded in his memoirs, "At midnight on January 27 the cease-fire went into effect and the killing stopped—at least for a time. I had always expected that I would feel an immense sense of relief and satisfaction when the war was finally ended. . . . I had no illusions about the fragile nature of the agreement or about the Communists' true motives in signing it." Nixon, having won election in the first place with promises that he would be able to conclude American participation early and "with honor," thereby finally separated himself from the conflict in Southeast Asia after overseeing an additional U.S. loss of 28,000 on top of the 30,000 already dead when he first took over in 1969. The agreement also provided for the return of 587 American POWs.

Just as fighting wound down, two of the earlier backers of the Asian war died in quick succession, Truman on December 26 and Johnson on January 22. Nixon attended both funerals and reaffirmed his sympathy for Johnson. "Seeking both guns and butter is a policy that works only in the very short term," he wrote in his tribute. "I think Johnson belatedly came to understand this, because through the four years of my first term I cannot recall an instance when he urged me to go forward with any of his Great Society programs."

Despite all the loss of life, Nixon did not gain much over what he had inherited from Johnson. Nor was there any substantial achievement over what Kissinger had appeared to settle for when making his "peace is at hand" statement in October. He had, however, withdrawn and immunized himself from charges of "cutting and running." What had not been achieved, to Thieu's consternation, was the removal of enemy troops from the South.

Instead, the treaty signed in Paris on January 27 was a compromise, one which left it up to both Vietnam governments to fight it out, without, of course, United States participation. But South Vietnam was wide open for the Chinese and Russians to bolster their client in Hanoi. Secretly, but important for a president already fighting for his own survival, was Nixon's assurance of an additional $3.25 billion in reparations for the reconstruction of North Vietnam. Equally empty was his promised military retaliation if Hanoi reneged on the treaty. With the American people long since weary of the war with its dubious objectives, Congress later refused to honor any such commitment. Nixon himself, in his waning days, was too distracted by his own problems to consider renewing any sort of Southeast Asia involvement.

Cambodian bombing continued for three months after the formal cease-fire, as the Americans fought to aid insurgents against the Khmer Rouge, but Congress prohibited further action in Southeast Asia altogether after August 15, which opened Cambodia to rule by Soviet-backed Communists. Unsurprisingly, what had really been achieved was a "decent interval" between the formal armistice and the North Vietnam's military takeover by April 1975, when remaining U.S. support personnel fled the embassy in Saigon.

Death of a Presidency

Nixon's second inaugural address, on January 20, 1973, coincided with the high point of his presidency, a period that included reaching out to the Chinese and the Russians as well as disengaging from the war. Unable, at that moment, to announce an official end to the fighting, he did what leaders do. He asked for "your prayers that in the years ahead I may have God's help in making decisions that are right for America, and I pray for your help so that together we may be worthy of our challenge."

Only one week later, he announced a cease-fire. A new Gallup poll showed the president with his highest approval rating yet, a solid 68 percent.

Less than two weeks earlier, with the election behind them and the war finally nearing its end, it fell to the chief judge of the United States District Court in Washington, Judge John Sirica, to open the trial of the five Watergate burglars, plus two other Plumbers, Gordon Liddy and Howard Hunt. Five of the men, including Hunt, pleaded guilty. Liddy and James W. McCord were convicted of conspiracy, burglary and wiretapping. Both had pleaded not guilty. One week later, on February 7, the case gained additional traction before the public when the Senate unanimously voted to create a special committee to investigate presidential campaign activities. With Democrats in the majority, the body was chaired by Senator Sam Ervin of North Carolina, renowned as a folksy country lawyer. Senator Howard Baker of Tennessee led the Republican minority.

Even before the Senate Watergate Committee began its hearings, McCord informed the judge that Attorney General John Mitchell and John Dean were responsible for denials that the burglars had White House connections. Haldeman had already advised Nixon that one of his more aggressive White House aides, Charles Colson, may also have been involved. "I simply can't believe," the president recorded for his diary, "based on my conversations with Colson, that he would have been so stupid as to think we could get such information through attempting to bug the other side." On March 22, in words that clearly showed Nixon's interest in hiding the affair, he told Mitchell that White House aides should "*stonewall, plead the Fifth Amendment, cover up or anything else.*" (emphasis supplied) The next day, Nixon's chief counsel, Dean, warned him, "We have a cancer within, close to the Presidency that is growing daily." A little more than three weeks later, Dean's eagerness for personal immunity from prosecution led him to begin to cooperate with the Watergate prosecutors.

Nixon's first major decision in the affair was delivered in a televised speech on April 30. After much hand wringing, and having decided to avoid explaining whether he was involved in Watergate, he announced the resignations of Haldeman and Ehrlichman, calling them two of the "finest public servants it has been my privilege to know." He also revealed that he had fired Dean. In tones reminiscent of his Checkers speech 20 years earlier, he explained that directly blaming them for Watergate "would be a cowardly thing to do," and that he, as the man at the top, had to "bear the responsibility," adding that he had to "maintain the integrity of the White House," which could not be guilty of a whitewash.

Creating much skepticism about "what he knew and when he knew it," as Senator Baker framed the problem during the hearings, the speech also left Nixon at a new low, too despondent to take phone calls, leaving that job to his wife, Pat. "I hope I don't wake up in the morning," Julie reported overhearing her father that night.

He was well into what he has described as eighteen months of "nightmare harassment," not only by Ervin digging for any possible clue of responsibility or cover-up, but also by the IRS, Congress's General Account Office, and the Miami district attorney. Their main target was the 1972 campaign contribution of the Hughes organization, kept in a safe-deposit box in Bebe Rebozo's bank. Denying that Bebe had even mentioned the money to him at the time it was given, wanting to avoid "a repetition of the loan to Donald Nixon," his brother, he thought of holding on to it until after the campaign for the liquidation of deficits that had been incurred, or perhaps for the upcoming congressional campaign in 1974. But the money was returned in June 1973.

Attorney General Richard Kleindienst resigned. His replacement was a liberal Massachusetts Republican, Eliot Richardson. Richardson then announced the appointment of his former Harvard Law School professor, Archibald Cox, who also served as solicitor general during the Kennedy presidency, as the Justice Department's special prosecutor for Watergate.

On May 18, the Senate Watergate Committee began nationally televised hearings, with about 80 percent of the American public tuned in at one time or another. With their star witness, Dean, due to testify, the White House, facing an additional embarrassment, was granted a request that Irvin postpone Dean's appearance. A new Gallup poll had already shown Nixon's approval ratings continuing to drop, now down to 45 percent from the 68 of just two months earlier.

* * *

Nixon, increasingly absorbed with foreign policy, embraced the continuing arms control process. Brezhnev's February 1973 letter to Nixon had suggested moving ahead with the summit. His agenda was relatively specific: the peaceful use of nuclear energy, and agreements on such economic issues as trade, along with such other matters as force reductions in Europe and the contentious Middle East. The overture came as a welcome refocusing for Nixon.

Arriving in the United States in June, in the midst of continued damning Watergate news with or without Dean's testimony, the Russian leader dropped in at such presidential venues as Camp David and San Clemente, in addition to the White House. The two leaders—Nixon going along largely to satisfy Brezhnev's needs—worked out an innocuous but highly heralded Agreement for the Prevention of Nuclear War. Vowing that each party would "refrain from the threat or use of force against the other Party," it put forth a document that was "almost entirely dependent on how it was regarded, interpreted, and applied, inasmuch as it dealt with actions in terms of purpose and intention," as diplomatic historian Raymond Garthoff has put it. About as effective as the utopian antiwar agreements of the 1920s, the price was right for Nixon. He and his Russian counterpart also dickered over precise ceilings on intercontinental ballistic missiles and nuclear warheads. The upshot was no match for what Nixon had once accomplished in Moscow. Moreover, with Watergate as the major distraction, the president left more and more of the heavy lifting to Kissinger. His distinguished visitors from the Kremlin understood that Nixon "clearly needed a success."

* * *

With Brezhnev out of the way, Dean went before the national cameras on June 25. As a fascinated nation sat through his seven-hour monotone, he read his 235-page opening statement. He reported that the president knew about the cover-up from the start. Nixon, according to the young counselor, had even tried to place his attorney general, Mitchell, as his fall guy; the attorney general, the nation's chief law enforcement officer, had paid hush money to Hunt. Dean's sweeping, authentic sounding statement, bolstered by details and specific dates, included blanket indictments of Haldeman, Ehrlichman, and Colson, and gave an astonished nation a portrait of a White House fully engaged in illegal actions. Even without prosecutorial hard evidence, the scandal had been brought to a new level. "Slowly, steadily," Dean wrote, "I would climb toward the moral abyss of the President's inner circle until I finally fell into it, thinking I had made it to the top just as I began to realize I had actually touched bottom."

Nixon tuned out, avoiding both radio and television, and secluded himself in his seaside home, La Grande Pacifica, at San Clemente. It took great personal willpower—something he often demonstrated during his critical period—to harden himself in the face of impending disaster. More and more, according to several accounts, not least of all Kissinger's, he turned to vodka martinis or gin, but sometimes bourbon or scotch. It "didn't take much to get him well-oiled," noted the president's old friend and law colleague, Len Garment. Eisenhower's younger brother, Milton, recalled that Nixon downed six martinis before dinner while in Moscow in 1959. How serious Nixon's drinking was always remained somewhat vague, although Kissinger famously referred to him as "my drunken friend." Years later, when the White House tapes were being transcribed, National Archives researchers could hear the clink of glass and slurred, rambling speech. He faced his greatest crisis, then, with a combination of the human need to escape from reality and the strength that seemed to energize him when confronted with disaster. After all, even before Dean's battle for his own immunity, the possibility of impeachment had become far less remote. One could only pray for the American presidency, hopefully to be spared having the office itself associated with the misdeeds or cover-ups.

* * *

In August, the frustrated Rogers gave up on his infuriating stint as secretary of state. Nixon, his old friend, had embarrassed him from the start of the administration; he once told a group of White House advisers that he would like the kind of relationship with a yet-to-be-appointed department head that would resemble the one in foreign affairs that he had with Kissinger, overlooking Rogers. "I don't think my father ever knew how much Kissinger was hurting Rogers," Nixon's daughter, Julie, explained in 1986. Multiple embarrassments, reminiscent of George H. W. Bush's experience at the United Nations during the diplomacy concerning China and Formosa, undermined Rogers. More recently, Kissinger delivered a major address devoted to European solidarity without even briefing him. His patience must have reached the boiling point in June when he was forced to confess before a meeting of NATO ambassadors that he had no idea "what consultations Dr. Kissinger had in mind" when the latter referred to an arms limitation agreement. When Rogers finally did quit, the president lost little time in naming Kissinger as his successor. The move only confirmed that he had clearly served not only as the adviser on national security affairs but also as a de facto secretary of state. Rogers remained embittered, pained not only by Kissinger but by his old friend and boss. Kissinger, for his part, considered Rogers ill informed, hopelessly dominated by the State Department, and personally vain. Nixon worried about having to live with a "psychopathic" Rogers, and Haldeman feared that if Kissinger "wins the battle with Rogers" he might not be "livable with afterwards," according to historian Robert Dallek's reading of recorded conversations.

The Russians, meanwhile, found a possible indication of the limitations of détente. Only ten days earlier, the latest American Cold War covert operation had reached its payoff with the death of Chile's president, Salvador Allende. Having done everything except use military force to keep the avowed Marxist from coming to power in Santiago, the CIA had facilitated the toppling of the duly-elected president.

With Nixon in Key Biscayne almost overwhelmed by legal problems, Kissinger's hand strengthened. The news from the Middle East reported that Israel was under siege, fighting, as it soon became clear, for its survival. A two-pronged drive by Egyptian troops across the Suez Canal in the south and by Syrian forces in the Golan Heights, was launched on Yom Kippur, the most sacred Jewish holy day; it threatened disaster, with untold possible consequences. Nixon had earlier advised Kissinger to be tough on the little nation, which was eager to hold on to the territorial gains made during the Six-Day War in 1967. Be so "pro-Israel that the oil states" would "break ranks," Nixon later advised his secretary of state, then flew back to Washington on October 10. He had plainly spelled out the administration's Hobson's choice, to steer carefully between the Jewish state and the oil-rich Arabs.

Much has been made of the Nixon-Kissinger management. Their respective claims to statesmanship were most pointed when they each later wanted the world to know how they helped salvage Israel from near defeat during the October war, with massive eleventh-hour airlifts of crucial supplies, 550 sorties in all, more armaments in two weeks than had bailed out Berlin in 1948–1949. As the transports from America unloaded their goods of war, Israelis sang "God Bless America," and Nixon became their national hero.

Near the end of the month, with the fighting over and the Israelis having regained the initiative, including reoccupying the Golan Heights, a dramatic highlight came when a message from Brezhnev urged the United States to participate with the Russians in jointly sending troops to rescue Egypt's trapped Third Army in the Sinai Desert. Failing that kind of cooperation, Kissinger's message implied, Moscow would send its own troops, a unilateral move that Kissinger considered as "one of the most serious challenges to an American President by a Soviet leader." Nothing had been as potentially explosive, he thought, since the Cuban missile crisis of 1962.

Accounts of the period invariably describe a lame duck president with falling rates of approval and seeking his own escapes. His "authority was deteriorating daily," Kissinger has written. Not until some three and a half hours after news about the start of fighting did Kissinger inform Nixon.

One of the most potentially fateful decisions virtually placed the nation's war-making power beyond presidential or congressional authority, into the hands of the secretary of state. While Nixon slept, Kissinger took charge with six other national security officials and issued a defiant, arguably bellicose, worldwide alert. American forces everywhere were placed at readiness for a showdown, creating a war footing. As Dallek describes it, "they were setting policy in a dangerous international crisis, and coming to a decision that should have rested with the president. . . ."

The only credit for Nixon's possible contribution to that order comes from Nixon. Only Nixon's personal account implies that he was involved. Fortunately, Brezhnev, as it turned out, was hardly about to risk a great-power war. But the constitutional implications of the "alert" remained.

The danger soon passed, with a UN-sponsored ceasefire ending the conflict on October 27, and a 7,000-man international force was deployed to ensure the peace. The fight gave Israel its most effective lifeline since the 1967 war, rescuing a nation desperate to preserve its post-Holocaust legitimacy. Many years later, an American newspaper, the *Jewish Press*, hailed Nixon as "The 'Anti-Semite' Who Saved Israel."

Kissinger went on from there to a month-long shuttle between Cairo and Jerusalem, effectively excluding the Russians, while the American public reeled under an oil embargo crisis. Imposed as a retaliatory strike for U.S. support of Israel by the Arab members of the Oil Producing Countries (OPEC), the retribution led to widespread gas shortages and high prices. Long lines for refills were common at pumps throughout many of the country's 220,000 service stations. Many found themselves depleted and forced to close, leaving Americans temporarily stripped of their freedom to drive, one of their "inalienable rights." The embargo, which was not lifted until March 18, compounded the effects of inflation. "Probably at no time in our nation," George Gallup told a conference of Republican governors, "have people felt more frustrated and skeptical of their government." Voters kept telling pollsters that they were more worried about prices than about scandals in Washington.

* * *

Some people, Nixon later wrote, thought he was "in a state of mental overload." One of the major tests of the presidency—any presidency—is the ability to deal with a multitude of issues simultaneously. Nixon had no such problem.

But in October, events almost got out of hand. Ervin's committee produced the almost casual revelation that Nixon had routinely taped telephone calls to the Oval Office and, indeed, voices in the office itself. Kennedy and Johnson had their own recording devices, and, in 1971, Nixon told Haldeman that he also wanted one. To be voice activated and capable of capturing sounds both from telephones and from within the Oval Office and the Cabinet Room, they would give Nixon a record of his presidency. On August 29, Judge Sirica ordered the president to turn over nine of the tapes for private review. The president, fighting for the life of his administration, held back, claiming immunity in the form of "executive privilege." Executive power, he and his attorneys held, immunized the president from having to share documentary material with other branches of government.

Nixon's mounting contempt for his vice president was well known to insiders. But Agnew suddenly posed a real problem. Already charged with taking kickbacks from road construction contractors during his governorship, Agnew pleaded *nolo contendere* (no contest) in a federal courtroom in Baltimore to a charge of federal income tax evasion. He resigned from his office almost immediately.

Acting in accordance with the Twenty-fifth Amendment providing for the filling of vice presidential vacancies, Nixon nominated the Republican house minority leader, Gerald Ford, his loyal longtime friend and colleague. The affable Ford was certain to win quick confirmation. The president had deftly avoided a battle he did not need.

He had his hands full over the tapes. One of his pals, Bob Abplanalp, the aerosol valve magnate, said he should have soaked them in kerosene and lit a bonfire. Once the availability of the evidence became known, of course, it was too late; Nixon needed them for his own record, presumably for presidential memoirs, but potentially, according to Colson, also for exculpatory material that might eventually defend him against charges from Haldeman and Ehrlichman. With the tapes very much alive, however, a little minuet was played out that summer with Judge Sirica's order upheld by the U.S. Circuit Court of Appeals for the District of Columbia, and Nixon offering a compromise solution: He would hear the tapes and release summaries. The rejection of that scheme by the special prosecutor, Cox, quickly created an impasse.

Also under simultaneous inspection, and all lumped together as "Watergate," were the president's tax returns and questions about the legitimacy of using government funds for improvements to the San Clemente and Key Biscayne properties. The Nixons were convinced his "tormentors" went after such targets because of the lack of sufficient other evidence to impeach him. However one may weigh that as a factor, there is no question that the president only made more enemies by his impoundment of funds, refusing to spend $30 billion worth of congressional appropriations. "Nixon impounded, impounded, and vetoed," Treasury Secretary William Simon later complained in a 1984 interview. "We didn't lose the impoundments on the impoundment issue. We lost it on the Watergate issue."

The biggest blowup, however, and the one that brought the Watergate affair to its most sensational heights, was the brouhaha that came to be known as the "Saturday night massacre."

* * *

In that battle over subpoenas and pleas of executive privilege, which had finally been denied by the Supreme Court, Nixon fired Cox, initiating the so-called "Saturday night massacre" that featured the protest resignations of Attorney General Elliot Richardson and his deputy William Ruckelshaus. The public had begun to realize that the whole matter was not trivial. After the Cox firing, a Gallup poll showed that the president's approval rating was down to an astonishing 17 percent.

With the crisis deepening, Nixon finally responded to court orders to release the tapes. But he did so in measured segments. Much of the public that had been inattentive until then was upset when the frequent appearance of the phrase "expletive deleted" in the transcripts suggested heavy use of profanity in the White House. Equally dramatic was the revelation in November that eighteen and a half minutes of a key tape were mysteriously erased, perhaps inadvertently by his long-time secretary Rosemary Woods, perhaps by an electronic glitch, perhaps even by Nixon, the gadgetry-challenged man. Whatever, the matter remains unresolved.

In February 1974, unknown to the press until June, secret hearings by a Watergate grand jury, catching even the House Judiciary Committee by surprise, named Nixon as an un-indicted co-conspirator in the possible attempt to cover up the Watergate burglary. Indicted at the same time were Bob Haldeman, John Mitchell, John Ehrlichman, White House aide Gordon C. Strachen, Assistant Attorney General Robert Mardian, and Kenneth Parkinson, chief counsel of CREEP. Haldeman, Ehrlichman, and Mitchell later served prison sentences.

* * *

The presidential plea that "one year of Watergate is enough" seemed ludicrous. Nixon undertook a whirlwind, five-nation presidential tour through the Middle East from June 10 to 19, 1974. Impeachment hearings under way in the House and conflicts over the tapes were still unresolved, but news about the indictment reached the public only three days before he left the country. The trip not only satisfied his interests and growing self-image as a worldly statesman, but was a welcome escape from Washington and his tormentors. He was greeted like a hero by some 100,000 in Jerusalem, and cheered by flag-waving crowds in Cairo standing along the long drive from the airport shouting "Nix-son." Except for a few discordant signs in Israel, references to Watergate and a reaction to anti-Semitic comments recorded on the tapes with the reminder that "We Are All Jew Boys," his presidential standing felt unchallenged, exactly the respect due a chief executive of the United States. His Egyptian visit even resulted in a tangible achievement, nuclear cooperation agreement with President Anwar el-Sadat.

Sometimes it was *good* to be president. An appreciative *New York Times* columnist, James Reston, exulted after he got home: "It is a tribute to the Nixon Administration and the Congress that despite all their differences over Watergate, inflation, jobs, prices, and taxes, they have not forgotten their common responsibilities to the larger questions of world order."

The battle continued to be waged in the courts, the Congress, and the press. That summer, the House Judiciary Committee agreed to three resolutions of impeachment, for obstruction of justice, abuse of presidential powers, and violation by the president of his oath of office. With the White House already besieged, the Oval Office tapes were released.

Finally, the evidence everybody had been looking for became public. The so-called "smoking gun" was on the tape of June 23, 1972, recorded only days after the break-in. Nixon could clearly be heard directing the cover-up by telling Haldeman to get the FBI to stop its investigation. At that point, the question came down to a matter of resignation or impeachment.

On August 7, Nixon received a three-man delegation of Republican leaders, Barry Goldwater and John Rhodes of Arizona, and Hugh Scott of Pennsylvania. The final decision remained in his hands. But the outlook, they told the president, was "very gloomy" and "distressing." His support in the Senate to counter an impeachment resolution was, at best, down to ten.

With no chance to avoid impeachment, and his popular support below 30 percent, Nixon announced that he would resign at noon the next day. On August 9, after a poignant informal farewell address to his family and the White House staff, Nixon flew back to San Clemente. Gerald Ford became the thirty-eighth president, and the first to be unelected. "Our long national nightmare is over," he declared.

One month later, on September 8, President Ford dropped a Sunday morning bombshell by announcing that he had pardoned Nixon. That stroke of his pen, which became more understandable as time went by, probably destroyed his chance to be elected in his own right.

Nixon's supporters generally argued that a trial would have put both the ex-president and the nation through an extended trauma. Ford's own presidency would have been choked by months of testimony and litigation. Nixon, they also held, had already paid a "sufficient" price for the actions.

Still, the pardon was unfortunate in several ways. Although Nixon in effect acknowledged his guilt by accepting it, the move was too premature for the airing of information that may have done much to sweep aside collateral allegations and suspicions. Nixon's argument that he was guilty of little that had not been done by his predecessors would have received a badly needed hearing. He would, at the same time, have been able to allay widely held suspicions of a power grab, which even included such fantastic rumors as a plot to cancel the presidential election of 1972.

A joint survey conducted by *Newsweek* and ABC News on the tenth anniversary of the break-in showed continuing confusion about what had really happened. More Americans, 10 percent more than on the day of Nixon's resignation, were convinced that he should have resigned. A majority, 56 percent, regretted that he had not been made to stand trial. A full cross-examination, which would have been possible only by placing Nixon himself on the witness stand, could have done much to shed light on notions that he was merely the victim of what British historian Paul Johnson has called "the first media Putsch in history." Admittedly, the cost of such intelligence would have been great, but a free society had the right to consider the administration's malfeasance in its proper perspective.

The hostile climate within the White House, as the tapes confirm, was unquestionably of Nixon's doing. Subsequent revelations, including information from Haldeman's diary, have deepened what we can understand about his negative demeanor, paranoia, and even his personal involvement. Ideas were planted and their execution left to the aggressive and adventurous. Nixon himself later admitted, on a national television interview conducted by David Frost on May 4, 1977, that he had "let the American people down" by aiding the cover-up. He had, in addition, through the telltale tapes, "fallen on his own sword."

The known recordings make it impossible to regard him as an innocent victim. More than once, Nixon's own voice confirmed his role in, at least, the cover-up. The concept of a Brookings break-in was clearly his. "Look," the president suggested more than once, "breaking and entering and so forth, without accomplishing it, is not a hell of a lot of crime." Insights from Haldeman and even unsubstantiated remarks from such sources as Martha Mitchell and Jeb Magruder, in addition to a close reading of the so-far released tapes, makes it all too clear that such activities were consistent with the kind of behavior tolerated, if not encouraged, by his presidency while fully convinced about protecting "national security." Unquestionably, Nixon's eagerness for politically useful information linking Larry O'Brien to Howard Hughes was well understood by those with access to the Oval Office. He needed to win regardless of the price.

Other circumstances may well have played a role in forcing the president out, certainly in weakening his hand. The worsening inflation of 1973, with meat prices ballooning by an annual rate of 75 percent by February, further agitated public opinion. Added to such factors were the Arab oil cartel's escalating prices, economic weaknesses traceable to the Johnson administration. Kept relatively level by the wage-price controls, the cost-of-living index shot upward after the lid was lifted. The president chose to impose a second freeze, or stage of controls, in 1973, but it was not enough to contain inflation and heightened the public's distress. With energy prices leading the way to an incredible annual rate of 72 percent by the winter quarter of 1974, in the aftermath of the OPEC retribution for the U.S. support of Israel during the Yom Kippur War, inflation zoomed to its highest peacetime peak in American history. With a substantial amount of the public also believing that the president was too cozy with the major oil companies, and rounds of shortages and long lines of motorists trying to fill their tanks, Nixon's approval rating dropped to 29 percent at the start of 1974.

The best way to understand Watergate is through an understanding of the culture of the Cold War, and the best way to gauge Nixon's presidency is to understand his approach to foreign relations between the United States and the rest of the world. Domestic policy was his route to power; to paraphrase Machiavelli, the art of gaining power was political, the art of implementing that power to assert his stamp on the U.S. and the world and, of course, his legacy, was through realpolitik leadership in the ongoing crisis with the Soviet Union, which carried over to Southeast Asia; hence, dealing with the situation in Vietnam and "playing the China card." As Nixon pointed out in a 1988 interview, the American people do not necessarily punish corruption, but they do react to pocketbook issues. When a public opinion poll asked, more than a year after the burglars broke in, to name the nation's worst problem, 89 percent said the high cost of living, 14 percent said Watergate and political corruption.

With the fighting in the past, and the presidency on the defensive, there were two attempts to reassert congressional power. First, the Democratic majority helped lead to a cut-off of further funding for the war. Then, in a further move to tie the hands of the impaired commander-in-chief, Congress, in November 1973, overrode a Nixon veto by passing the War Powers Resolution, which was designed to limit White House war-making powers. The effort to diminish such presidential constitutional authority by enhancing the congressional role was designed, in effect, to convert the commander-in-chief into what the *Wall Street Journal* pointed out was really a "committee in chief." The resolution, passed with much enthusiasm by those concerned with limiting the war-making powers of what critics had denounced as Nixon's "imperial presidency," proved to be but a feeble revision of the constitutional question of presidential versus congressional authorization. Its principal author, Senator Jacob K. Javits of New York, was prophetic when he wrote the following: "Whether or not the Resolution is enforced will . . . depend upon the determination of Congress to stand up and fight for its constitutional rights respecting war . . . and the power of the President to get the country to side with him politically and thus make the Resolution a nullity . . ." Nevertheless, the ambiguity of which branch has the primary authority to go to war remains, and it is hard to imagine any president, let alone Nixon, signing into law what he would clearly regard as an infringement. Nixon was only a bystander when Congress then also liquidated all monies for fighting in Southeast Asia.

* * *

Long before his death, analysts had already had their say, drawn in part by such comments as the one made by Ehrlichman a dozen years earlier. Nixon was "enormously complex," said the former adviser for domestic affairs and one of the men discredited by Watergate. "The big danger in writing the history of Richard Nixon is oversimplifying him." "There were constantly new Nixons because of his awareness that he was catering to a new mood." Kissinger once asked, "Can you imagine what this man would have been had somebody loved him?"

Others saw him purely in terms of power, ambition, and political cynicism; in many ways an enigma, a subject attractive to an array of psycho-biographers. He was, many who knew him agreed, an outsider, suspicious of people, and, in Ehrlichman's words, "'paradoxical,' the strangest combination of any man I ever heard of." Nixon economist Herb Stein said over lunch at the American Enterprise Institute, that "Cynicism is strong in Nixon," a man who continued to see himself as a protector of the free market.

Yet, to more recent analysts, writers like Tom Wicker, Joan Hoff, and David Greenberg, Nixon contributed importantly to the enabling of desegregation, domestic reforms and a concept of New Federalism that exceeded his accomplishments in foreign affairs, and established "the high-water mark of post–New Deal activism." Thus, especially to many who have studied him, Nixon remains an enigma. The diplomatic initiatives of the "cold warrior," in the end, especially with China and the USSR, to say nothing of his nuclear accords, went far toward achieving the successful resolution of the great conflict that had pitted East against West. Indeed, the president widely credited for ending the Cold War, Ronald Reagan, periodically turned to Nixon as a foreign policy consultant, which suited him fine. In his retirement, he liked to think of himself as an elder statesman.

Nixon clearly had his "establishment" moments, and they could be found at the core of his psyche. Nearly everything about Nixon was conservative—favoring fountain pens, three-piece business suits, and ties even in intimate family situations. A photograph once caught him walking on the beach at San Clemente in wing-tipped shoes. He never departed from traditional family relationships, even within the reality of a difficult marriage. Along with most of his fellow Americans, Nixon aspired to the accoutrements of a bourgeoisie lifestyle, and the company of those who made their own fortunes.

Historians and biographers, it seems, have been unable to say enough about him. The grand total has been nearing 1,000 volumes. Many, including the psycho-biographers, don't seem to have any more credible basis for their analyses than what they could get from the media and his public reputation.

The question of who was really behind him came up often. He was totally pragmatic, said Ehrlichman in a 1985 interview. "If the anti-freeway people would support him, he would be anti-freeway." Nixon's rise to the

White House coincided not only with the petering out of Depression-era politics but with the advanced assimilation of the European immigration that had largely dissipated after the 1920s. Thus, the new ethnicity became a force not of newcomers but of second- and third-generation Americans who were ready to leave behind the "world of their fathers" ideologically while retaining their cultural identities. From the start of his campaign for the presidency until the attempted assassination of George Wallace in Laurel, Maryland, for example, understanding the underlying discontent of middle-class Americans who labored for a living, he renounced his earlier sympathies and understanding of the civil rights movement. Virtually making himself over, he adopted class appeals and competed with the racist rhetoric of Wallace, although more respectably and with matching tones of populism.

In his final book, *Beyond Peace*, Nixon wrote, "Millions came to our shores because America stood for free elections, free people, free markets, freedom of expression, and freedom of religion. Never has it been more important for us to demonstrate to the rest of the world the power of this idea." And then he went on to conclude, "We must improve ourselves at home so that our example shines more brightly abroad." Richard Nixon, the enigmatic traditionalist, conservative and populist, was, in the end, an idealist, but also, in his mind, an intellectual realist; lacking the birthright legacy that boosted so many of his rivals in American politics, his success depended on his guts, his wiles, and his ability, as he emphasized in his *Six Crises*, to mobilize strength in the face of challenges. Indictment over Watergate revealed *the establishment* lashing out for his presumptuous climb to the top. He did not, as journalist Victor Lasky argued in defense of Nixon, *invent* the excesses revealed by the scandal. The man regarded as one of the most brilliant and insightful politicians of his time, never really accepted responsibility for helping to undermine the nation's constitutional foundation and the integrity of the presidency.

* * *

On April 24, 1994, 81 years after his birth, Richard Nixon died two days after a massive stroke. He was buried in Yorba Linda, on the grounds of the Richard M. Nixon Library and Birthplace. Beyond the gate of Nixon's final resting place, alongside the grave of Pat, who had died a year earlier, hundreds of men, women, and children stood or sat on folding chairs lining the boulevard so they could watch the presidential cortege. Hours later, with the ceremony over and the skies threatening, the onlookers remained fixed in place, communing with history, eager for any glimpse of those who had as much as touched the president.

Study and Discussion Questions

Chapter 1: A Quaker from Whittier

1. What elements in Nixon's early background foreshadowed his future?

2. What turned out to be Nixon's most significant wartime experiences?

3. Would you say that his early history broadened his background or confirmed his prejudices?

4. What was the author's basic purpose in writing this chapter?

Chapter 2: From Whittier to Washington

1. Why did Herman Perry invite Nixon to run?

2. What kind of people constituted the base of Nixon's support?

3. How did he differ from Jerry Voorhis?

4. What was distinctive about Nixon's 1946 campaign and election?

Chapter 3: You're My Boy

1. What developments helped to build Nixon's national prominence before the 1952 presidential campaign?

2. Why did Eisenhower choose Nixon to become his running mate?

3. What kinds of appeal did Nixon make in his Checkers speech?

4. What can account for the strengthening of "Republican hard-liners?"

5. What were the limits to Nixon's bipartisanship during the early Cold War years?

6. Why did so many Americans go for Eisenhower in 1952?

7. How did Nixon distinguish himself during the debates about China?

Chapter 4: Vice President

1. What enabled Nixon to become such a strong vice president?

2. Why did he later regret the Suez affair?

3. How did his experiences under Eisenhower reinforce his image as a controversial figure?

4. In what ways did Nixon's vice presidency become a learning experience?

Chapter 5: Defeat

1. What does *Six Crises* reveal about Nixon's personality?

2. To what would you attribute Nixon's loss in 1960?

3. What did his gubernatorial campaign in 1962 reveal about Nixon?

Chapter 6: Resurrection

1. What were the significant national changes that took place while Nixon practiced law in New York?

2. Why was the war in Vietnam such a dilemma to Nixon as a presidential candidate? How did he propose to deal with it if elected?

3. Do you think that the Nixon campaign truly followed a "national" strategy in 1968, as his people said, or a "Southern" strategy, as others believed?

4. How did the Democrats weaken themselves?

5. Should Nixon be condemned for the Chennault affair?

Chapter 7: A Governing Center

1. What does this chapter tell us about Nixon's organization of the office of the President?

2. What does it tell us about his social outlook?

Chapter 8: Nixon and the World

1. How did Nixon handle the antiwar movement?

2. What was Agnew's role?

3. What do you think he meant by "positive polarization?"

4. What do we know about Nixon's inner thoughts during that turbulent period?

5. How did Nixon increase the level of presidential surveillance?

6. What did Nixon learn about the importance of images?

7. How should we characterize Nixon's handling of the civil rights movement?

Chapter 9: Alone in the Lincoln Sitting Room

1. What were the major elements in the administration's program to curb inflation?

2. Do you agree with Nixon that the "China opening" would have happened even without a war in Vietnam?

3. What safeguards did the Nixon administration take to prepare for re-election in 1972?

Chapter 10: A "Third-Rate" Burglary

1. Why was the Watergate break-in a relatively inconsequential issue during the 1972 election campaign?

2. How did Nixon reach out to strengthen his support from conservatives?

3. Of what importance was ending the draft?

4. What were the most significant aspects of the 1972 election?

Chapter 11: Death of a Presidency

1. What were the steps that led up to the "death of a presidency?"

2. How justifiable was the rationale that White House transgressions did not "start with Watergate"?

3. Why has public opinion shifted about President Ford's pardon of Nixon?

4. What elements helped make Nixon an enigmatic figure?

A Note on the Sources

The starting place for researchers trying to fathom the Nixon years is the Richard Nixon Library & Birthplace at Yorba Linda, California, one of the most recent additions to the National Archives, and certain to gain in importance as a major source. The Library has Finding aids available online at http://nixon foundation.org, along with http://nixon.archives.gov/index.php.

Even without the material that became available later, including the White House tapes, Stephen E. Ambrose's three-volume biography (New York: Simon & Schuster, 1987–1991) remains indispensable, as is Nixon's own *RN: The Memoirs of Richard Nixon* (New York: Grosset & Dunlap, 1978). Also highly useful is Richard Reeves's more recent chronological one-volume account, *President Nixon* (New York: Grosset & Dunlap, 2001). The first part of a projected multi-volume biography, Irwin F. Gellman's *The Contender: Richard Nixon, The Congress Years 1946–1952* (New York: The Free Press, 1999), indicates the coming of a major, careful study. Anthony Summers, *The Arrogance of Power: The Secret World of Richard Nixon* (New York: Viking Press, 2000), is highly critical, but helpful, if used with care. Succinct but reliable studies can be found in Melvin Small, *The Presidency of Richard Nixon* (Lawrence, Kans.: University Press of Kansas, 1999), and Robert Mason, *Richard Nixon and the Quest for a New Majority* (Chapel Hill, N.C.: University of North Carolina Press, 2004). For a valuable oral history portrait of the thirty-seventh president, see Deborah Hart Strober and Gerald S. Strober (eds.), *The Nixon Presidency: An Oral History of the Era* (Washington, D.C.: Brassey's Inc., 1994).

Insightful interpretations are available from David Green-berg's stimulating *Nixon's Shadow* (New York: Norton, 2003). Joan Hoff's *Nixon Reconsidered* (New York: Basic Books, 1994) is a provocative revisionist view arguing for the primacy of domestic policies as a key to an understanding of Nixon's ad-ministration. His own first book, published soon after he left the presidency, *Six Crises* (New York: Doubleday, 1962), is also surprisingly revealing.

Outstanding examples of the psycho-biographical treatments about Nixon are David Abrahamsen, *Nixon vs. Nixon: An Emo-tional Tragedy* (New York: Signet Books, 1978); Fawn Brodie, *Richard Nixon: The Shaping of His Character* (New York: Norton, 1981); and especially Bruce Mazlish's *In Search of Nixon* (New York: Basic Books, 1972). The first significant interpretive study, one that still stands up, is Garry Wills, *Nixon Agonistes: The Crisis of the Self-Made Man* (Boston: Houghton Mifflin, 1970). Jonathan Schell, *The Time of Illusion* (New York: Vintage Books, 1976), is also surprisingly fresh. Journalist Jules Witcover has recently chronicled the odd relationship between Nixon and his vice president in *The Short and Unhappy Marriage of Richard Nixon and Spiro Agnew* (New York: Public Affairs, 2007).

For more partisan versions, Julie Nixon Eisenhower's under-standably sympathetic account, *Pat Nixon: The Untold Story* (New York: Simon & Schuster, 1986), and Jonathan Aitken's *Nixon: A Life* (Washington, D.C.: Regnery Publishing, 1993) should also be read. Tom Wicker, *One of Us: Richard Nixon and the American Dream* (New York: Random House, 1991), also understands the Nixon enigma.

Several views of the presidency from insiders include Ray-mond Price, *With Nixon* (New York: Viking Press, 1977); William Safire, *Before the Fall* (New York: Doubleday, 1975); John Ehrlichman, *Witness to Power: The Nixon Years* (New York: Simon & Schuster, 1982); and Herbert G. Klein, *Making It Perfectly Clear* (New York: Doubleday, 1980). But H. R. Haldeman's *The Haldeman Diaries: Inside the Nixon White House* (New York: Putnam, 1994) is required reading for any-body with a serious interest in that presidency. An excellent contemporary journalistic account is Rowland Evans, Jr., and

Robert D. Novak, *Nixon in the White House: The Frustration of Power* (New York: Random House, 1971).

In addition to the special access found in British journalist Aitken's account, better acquaintance with Nixon's global thoughts can be obtained by reading his own formidable volumes, *Leaders* (New York: Simon & Schuster, 1982); *1999: Victory Without War* (New York: Simon & Schuster, 1988); *No More Vietnams* (New Rochelle, N.Y.: Arbor House, 1985); *The Real War* (New York: Warner Books, 1980); *RN: The Memoirs of Richard Nixon* (New York: Grosset & Dunlap, 1978); *Six Crises* (New York: Doubleday, 1962); and *Beyond Peace* (New York: Random House, 1994). My own earlier work, *Richard Nixon and His America* (Boston: Little, Brown, 1990), also profited from access to the former president.

A close acquaintance with American politics during the Nixon years, especially at the grassroots level, although requiring patience, is available through a careful reading of the 1972 and 1974 volumes of *The Almanac of American Politics*, by Michael Barone, Grant Ujifusa, and Douglas Matthews (Boston: The National Journal, 1972, 1974). Their district-by-district reports and analyses are unmatched elsewhere. Douglas Brinkley's *Gerald R. Ford* (New York: Times Books, 2007) discusses the pardon and the Nixon-to-Ford transition. Five volumes of contemporary journalist Theodore H. White, some with day-by-day accounts, are still indispensable: *Breach of Faith: The Fall of Richard Nixon* (New York: Atheneum, 1975); *The Making of the President 1960* (New York: Atheneum, 1961); *The Making of the President 1964* (New York: Atheneum, 1965); *The Making of the President 1972* (New York: Atheneum, 1973); and *The Making of the President 1968* (New York: Atheneum, 1969).

Nixon's final post-presidential chief of staff, Monica Crowley, produced two books that convey her boss's thinking about geopolitics, *Nixon Off the Record* (New York: Random House, 1996) and *Nixon in Winter* (New York: Random House, 1998).

The iconic work on the Nixon administration's foreign policy is Arthur M. Schlesinger, Jr.'s *The Imperial Presidency* (Boston: Houghton Mifflin, 1973). Any informed study of the era's diplomacy signals that the quality of the Nixon–Henry

Kissinger relationship is worth a separate volume. Robert Dallek had done just that with his invaluable *Nixon and Kissinger: Partners in Power* (New York and San Francisco: HarperCollins, 2007), which is likely to become the definitive account of that relationship. Not to be overlooked is Henry Kissinger's *White House Years* (Boston: Little, Brown, 1979), together with Walter Isaacson, *Kissinger: A Biography* (New York: Simon & Schuster, 1992); Seymour Hersh, *The Price of Power* (New York: Summit Books, 1983); and such significant scholarly works as Raymond L. Garthoff, *Détente and Confrontation: American-Soviet Relations from Nixon to Reagan* (Washington, D.C.: The Brookings Institution, 1985); George C. Herring, *America's Longest War* (2nd ed., New York: Random House, 1986); Larry Berman, *Planning a Tragedy: The Americanization of the War in Vietnam* (New York: Norton, 1982); Jeffrey Kimball, *Nixon's Vietnam War* (Lawrence, Kans.: University Press of Kansas, 1998); David Kaiser, *American Tragedy* (Cambridge, Mass.: Belknap Press, 2000); Robert Litwak, *Détente and the Nixon Doctrine* (Cambridge, Mass.: Cambridge University Press, 1984); Melvin Small, *Johnson, Nixon and the Doves* (New Brunswick, N.J.: Rutgers University Press, 1988); Guenther Lewy, *America in Vietnam* (New York: Oxford University Press, 1978); Arnold R. Isaacs, *Without Honor* (Baltimore, Md.: Johns Hopkins University Press, 1983); and Seyom Brown, *The Faces of Power* (New York: Columbia University Press, 1983). For behind-the-scene dispatches, see Nguyen Tien Hung and Jerrold L. Schecter, *The Palace File* (New York: Harper & Row, 1986). A handy, concise, and readable analysis is provided in John L. Gaddis, *The Cold War: A New History* (New York: The Penguin Press, 1985). Still, even after all these years, the best introduction to the conflict will be found in Stanley Karnow, *Vietnam: A History* (New York: Viking, 1983). Other, more colorful views of Nixon and the world appear in Margaret MacMillan's richly detailed and insightful *Nixon and Mao: The Week That Changed the World* (New York: Random House, 2007), William Shawcross, *Sideshow: Kissinger, Nixon and the Destruction of Cambodia* (New York: Simon & Schuster, 1979), and Neil Sheehan, *A*

Bright Shining Lie: John Paul Van and America in Vietnam (New York: Random House, 1988). Sanford J. Unger, *The Papers and the Papers* (New York: Notable Trials Library, 1972), analyzes the episode that surrounded the publication of the Pentagon Papers.

Other significant accounts of what some have called the "Age of Nixon" include Jack Bass and Walter DeVries, *Transformation of Southern Politics: Social Change and Political Consequences Since 1943* (New York: Basic Books, 1976); Lewis Chester, Godfrey Hodgson, and Bruce Page, *An American Melodrama* (New York: Pantheon Books, 1969); Alan Crawford, *Thunder on the Right: The "New Right" and the Politics of Resentment* (New York: Random House, 1980); Elizabeth Drew, *Washington Journal: The Events of 1973–1974* (New York: Stein & Day, 1975); David Frost, *The Presidential Debate, 1968* (New York: Random House, 1968); Lewis L. Gould, *Grand Old Party: A History of the Republicans* (New York: Random House, 2003); Norman Mailer, *Some Honorable Men: Political Conventions 1960–1972.* (Boston: Trident Press, 1976); Ernest R. May and Janet Fraser (eds.), *Campaign '72: The Managers Speak* (Cambridge, Mass.: Harvard University Press, 1973); Joe McGinniss, *The Selling of the President 1968* (New York: Trident Press, 1968); Norman H. Nie, Sidney Verba, and John R. Petrocik, *The Changing American Voter* (Cambridge, Mass.: Harvard University Press, 1976); Kevin Phillips, *The Emerging Republican Majority* (New York: Arlington House, 1969); Ronald Radosh, *Divided They Fell: The Demise of the Democratic Party 1964–1996* (New York: The Free Press, 1996); William Rusher, *The Rise of the Right* (New York: Coward McCann, 1984); Richard M. Scammon and Ben J. Wattenberg, *The Real Majority* (New York: Coward McCann, 1970); A. James Reichley, *Conservatives in an Age of Change* (Washington, D.C.: The Brookings Institution, 1981), and David W. Reinhard, *The Republican Right Since 1945* (Lexington, Ky.: University Press of Kentucky, 1983). An important guide for a background to the shifts in American politics during the entire post-war era may be found in Thomas Byrne Edsall and Mary D. Edsall, *Chain Reaction: The Impact of Race, Rights, and Taxes on*

American Politics (New York: Norton, 1991). For a positive view of Nixon and civil rights, see Dean J. Kotlowski, *Nixon's Civil Rights: Politics, Principles and Policy* (Cambridge, Mass.: Harvard University Press, 2002). On ending the draft, see Robert K. Griffith, *The U.S. Army Transition to an All-Volunteer Force, 1968–1974* (Lexington, Ky.: University Press of Kentucky, 1997).

For the 1972 election, see Timothy Crouse, *The Boys on the Bus* (New York: Ballantine, 1973); Gary W. Hart, *Right From the Start: a Chronicle of the McGovern Campaign* (New York: Quadrangle, 1973); Ernest R. May and Janet Fraser, *Campaign '72: The Managers Speak* (Cambridge, Mass.: Harvard University Press, 1973); George McGovern, *An American Journey: Presidential Campaign Speeches of George McGovern*; (New York: Random House, 1974); Byron E. Shafer, *Quiet Revolution* (New York: Russell Sage Foundation, 1983); Hunter S. Thompson, *Fear and Loathing: On the Campaign Trail '72* (San Francisco: Allison & Busby, 1973); and Theodore H. White, *The Making of the President 1972* (New York: Atheneum, 1973).

For the Watergate scandals, a starting place for acquaintance with the scandals and their ramifications is the contemporary work by the two journalists who won fame for their reportage, Bob Woodward and Carl Bernstein, starting with *The End of a Presidency* (New York: Simon & Schuster, 1974), and followed by *All the President's Men* (New York: Simon & Schuster, 1974), and *The Final Days* (New York: Simon & Schuster, 1976). Woodward is the sole author of two more recent books, *Shadow* (New York: Simon & Schuster, 1999), which is especially useful for its description of the events that led to the Nixon pardon, and *The Secret Man* (New York: Simon & Schuster, 2005), an account of the man previously known as Deep Throat.

Stanley Kutler, *The Wars of Watergate* (New York: Alfred Knopf, 1992), is the most comprehensive scholarly account. An early but careful and readable report is contained in J. Anthony Lukas's *Nightmare: The Underside of the Nixon Years* (New York: Viking Press, 1976). For a more succinct but reliable overview, see Keith W. Olson, *Watergate* (Lawrence, Kans.: University Press of Kansas, 2003). For provocative, controversial accounts that fly in the face of conventional wisdom, see, especially, Len Colodny and Robert Gettlin, *Silent Coup* (New York: St. Martin's Press, 1991); Jim Hougan, *Secret Agenda: Watergate, Deep Throat and the CIA* (New York: Random House, 1984); and Michael Drosnin, *Citizen Hughes* (New York: Henry Holt, 1985).

In late 1993, the National Archives produced a compact disc containing a finding aid to the White House tapes recorded during the Nixon years. That oral record will long remain an essential primary source. A handy paperback volume containing contemporary reports may be found in a publication by the *New York Times*, *The End of a Presidency* (New York: Viking Press, 1974). Other works include R. W. Apple, Jr., et al., *The Watergate Hearings, Break-in and Cover-Up: Proceedings of the Senate Select Committee on Presidential Campaign Activities* as edited by the staff of the *New York Times* (New York: Viking Press, 1973); and Stanley I. Kutler (ed.), *Abuse of Power: The New Nixon Tapes* (New York: The Free Press, 1997), an edited selection of the tapes. Additional primary source material is available from Bruce Oudes (ed.), *From the President: Richard Nixon's Secret Files* (New York: Harper & Row, 1989).

The Internet also constitutes a handy source for information. Finding aids for the Nixon White House tapes are currently available from the Richard Nixon Library & Birthplace at Yorba Linda, California. See the library home page online at http://www.nixonfoundation.org, along with http://nixon.archives.gov/index.php.

Selective recently declassified documents are also becoming available online. The Web site for the U.S. State Department lists the published volumes of the Foreign Relations of the United States series through the Nixon years. It may be accessed at http://www.state.gov/r/pa/ho/frus/nixon/. Another site, http://www.c-span.org/executive/presidential/nixon.asp offers selective archival excerpts from the Nixon Presidential White House tapes as posted by C-SPAN.

Index